Language Arts Handbo
Grade Three
Table of Contents

www.svschoolsupply.com

Language Arts Handbook
Grade Three
Introduction

This book is designed to help review and reinforce the language skills that students will master in the third grade. It is a comprehensive handbook that addresses a broad range of the language concepts that students will encounter at this grade level. It can be used effectively as a tool to reinforce language skills at school or at home, or to keep skills sharp over extended vacations.

Organization

These activities are designed to reinforce the language skills that are important for students in the third grade. This book is divided into eight units: Grammar, Sentences, Vocabulary and Usage, Capitalization and Punctuation, Kinds of Writing, Paragraphs, Resource Materials and Research, and Reading Comprehension. Each section focuses on one or two related concepts, and assessment pages appear at the beginning of each unit to give teachers or parents the opportunity to gauge understanding and to signal if more practice is needed.

- **Grammar.** Several major parts of speech—nouns, verbs, adjectives, pronouns, compound words, and contractions—are defined, and students are given the opportunity for practice.

- **Sentences.** Students learn the parts of a sentence, the different kinds of sentences, how to join sentences, and how to write clear, descriptive sentences.

- **Vocabulary and Usage.** Students review synonyms, antonyms, prefixes, suffixes, homographs, homophones, abbreviations, and subject-verb agreement, and study common spelling problems.

- **Capitalization and Punctuation.** Students study the common uses of capitalization, such as the beginning of sentences, names of people, places, days, months, and titles. Students practice correct usage of the period, the question mark, the exclamation point, the comma, the colon, the apostrophe, underlines, and quotation marks.

- **Kinds of Writing.** Several common types of writing are reviewed, including story, poem, news story, magazine article, friendly letter, invitation, thank-you note, envelope address, journal entry, and book report.

- **Paragraphs.** Paragraphs are defined, and good paragraph writing is explained. Students examine the different types of paragraphs, including how-to, comparing, contrasting, information, defining, describing, opinion, and persuading, and work with each type.

- **Resource Materials and Research.** Students review the parts of a book, dictionary, encyclopedia, and map skills. Fiction and nonfiction writing is addressed. Students learn how to take notes, make outlines, write rough drafts and final research reports.

- **Reading Comprehension.** Important comprehension skills are practiced, including drawing conclusions, comparing, contrasting, classifying, identifying details, sequencing, cause and effect, judgments, summarizing, predicting outcomes, main idea, paraphrasing, distinguishing between reality and fantasy, and problems and solutions.

Use

This book is designed for independent use by students who have been introduced to the skills and concepts described. Copies of the activities can be given to individuals, pairs of students, or small groups for completion. They may be used as a center activity. If students are familiar with the content, the worksheets may also be used as homework.

To begin, determine the implementation that fits your students' needs and your classroom structure. The following plan suggests a format for this implementation.

1. **Explain** the purpose of the worksheets to your students. Let them know that these activities will be fun as well as helpful.

2. **Review** the mechanics of how you want the students to work with the activities. Do you want them to work in groups? Are the activities for homework?

3. **Decide** how you would like to use the assessments. They can be given before and after a unit to determine progress, or only after a unit to assess how well the concepts have been learned. Determine whether you will send the tests home or keep them in the students' portfolios.

4. **Introduce** students to the process and the purpose of the activities. Go over the directions. Work with children when they have difficulty. Work only a few pages at a time to avoid pressure.

5. **Do** a practice activity together.

Additional Notes

- **Parent Communication:** Send the Letter to Parents home with students so that parents will know what to expect and how they can best help their child.

- **Bulletin Board:** Display completed work to show student progress.

- **Assessments:** The first page of each unit is a unit assessment. You can use the assessments as diagnostic tools by administering them before children begin the activities. After children have completed each unit, let them retake the unit test to see the progress they have made. The assessments may be sent home or kept in portfolios for parent/teacher conferencing.

- **Center Activities:** Use the worksheets as a center activity to give students the opportunity to work cooperatively.

- **Have fun.** Working with these activities can be fun as well as meaningful for you and your students.

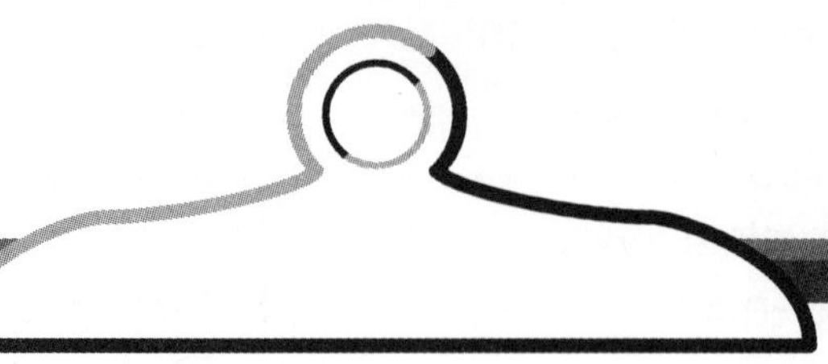

Dear Parent,

During this school year, our class will be using an activity book to reinforce the language skills that we are learning. By working together, we can be sure that your child not only masters these language skills but also becomes confident in his or her abilities.

From time to time, I may send home activity sheets. To help your child, please consider the following suggestions:

- Provide a quiet place to work.
- Go over the directions together.
- Encourage your child to do his or her best.
- Check the lesson when it is complete.
- Note improvements as well as problems.

Help your child maintain a positive attitude about the activities. Let your child know that each lesson provides an opportunity to have fun and to learn. Above all, enjoy this time you spend with your child. As your child's language skills develop, he or she will feel your support.

Thank you for your help.

Cordially,

Name ______________________ Date ____________

Unit One Assessment: Grammar

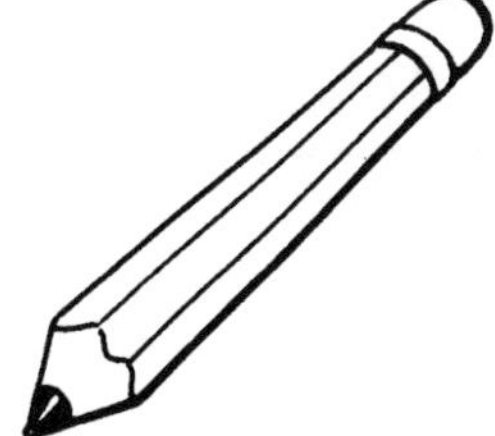

Choose one of the words from the box to name each of the underlined words.

common noun	proper noun	plural noun	pronoun
present tense verb	adjective	past tense verb	
possessive noun	contraction	compound word	

1. Many fruits are grown in the United States. ______________
2. This plant is a fern. ______________
3. They are the only ones left. ______________
4. That was a tasty meal. ______________
5. My mother bought me a coat. ______________
6. My dog's house is small. ______________
7. You can tell that it's a doghouse. ______________
8. Put your sunglasses on the shelf. ______________
9. Those daisies will look nice in a vase. ______________
10. Let's ride over to the park. ______________

Circle the linking verb in this sentence.

11. Sometimes the wind is dangerous.

Write the past tense of each verb.

12. come ______________
13. go ______________
14. eat ______________
15. begin ______________
16. think ______________
17. say ______________
18. take ______________
19. ring ______________
20. meet ______________

Name ______________________ Date ______________

Get the Nouns Down

☞ A **noun** is a word that names a person, place, or thing.

☞ A **common noun** names any person, place, or thing. It begins with a small letter.

girl **garden** **fruit**

☞ A **proper noun** names a special person, place, or thing. It begins with a capital letter.

Miss Pea **Greenwich** **Super Food Store**

Practice

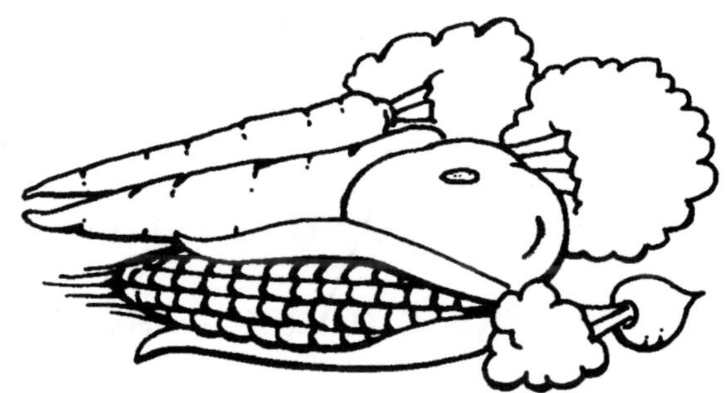

✎ Read each sentence. Then underline each common noun once and each proper noun twice.

1. Many fruits grow in the United States.
2. Many vegetables are grown in this country, too.
3. Much rice is grown in China.
4. Did you know that raisins are made from grapes?
5. Prunes are really dried plums.
6. There is a plant called a fern.
7. Much heather grows in the hills of Scotland.
8. Some cucumbers are used to make pickles.
9. Different potatoes are grown in Idaho and Ireland.
10. Large mangos are grown in Mexico.
11. A fruit grown in Hawaii is the pineapple.
12. In Indiana, corn and beans are grown.

Name ______________________ Date ______________

Nouns Abound

☞ A **singular noun** names one person, place, or thing.

girl **farm** **garden**

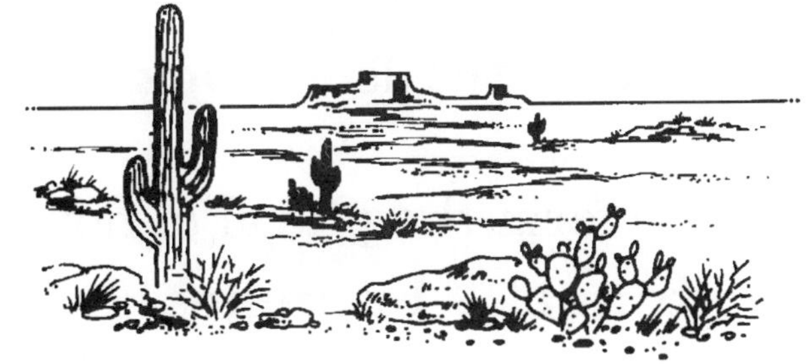

☞ A **plural noun** names more than one person, place, or thing.

flower—flowers
scratch—scratches
daisy—daisies
man—men
rock—rocks
branch—branches
fly—flies
cactus—cacti

Practice

✎ Complete each sentence correctly. Choose and circle the singular or plural form of each noun in ( ).

1. Papago (Indian, Indians) live in the desert.
2. We walked along a sandy (trail, trails).
3. A (hedgehog, hedgehogs) scampered across the trail.
4. The (cactus, cacti) were very tall.
5. They had long, sharp (spine, spines).
6. The (branch, branches) of the cacti reached to the sky.
7. Small (bunch, bunches) of flowers covered the cacti.
8. A nest was hidden in a (bush, bushes).
9. There were nine (egg, eggs) in the nest.
10. There were five (man, men) in the store.

Name ______________________________ Date ______________

More Than One Noun

☞ To form the plural of most nouns, add *s*.
trail—trails **rock—rocks**

☞ To form the plural of nouns ending in *s, x, ch*, or *sh,* add *es*.
branch—branches **bush—bushes**

☞ To form the plural of nouns ending with a consonant and *y*, change the *y* to *i* and add *es*.
beauty—beauties **family—families**

☞ A few nouns are the same in the singular and plural form.
deer—deer **sheep—sheep**

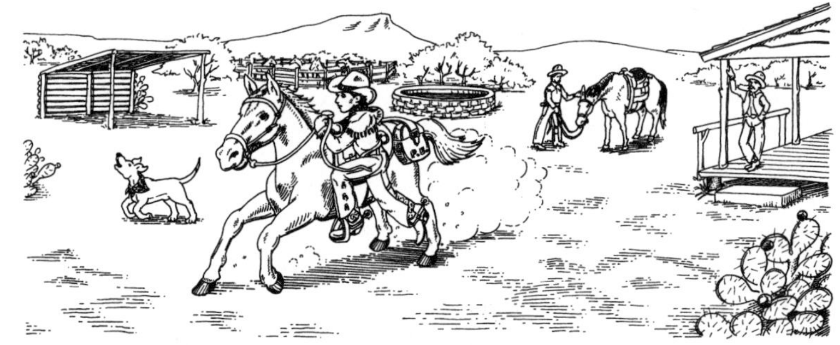

Practice

✎ Complete each sentence. Write the plural form of the noun in ( ) in the blank.

1. We went to visit some ________________. (friend)
2. Our friends live on two ________________. (ranch)
3. Our friends' grandmother tells great ________________. (story)
4. She knows how to sew lovely ________________. (dress)
5. The ________________ are so small and delicate. (stitch)
6. She also makes beautiful pins, called ________________, out of blue jewels. (brooch)
7. Some of the pins are shaped like ________________. (deer)
8. ________________ are also buying her pins. (Store)

Name ______________________________ Date ______________

That's My Noun!

☞ A **possessive noun** shows ownership, or possession.

The home of Lana seemed like a palace.

Lana's home seemed like a palace.

☞ Add an apostrophe (') and an *s* to singular nouns to show possession.

Cara's pet is very happy in her new home.

☞ Add an apostrophe (') to plural nouns that end in *s* to show possession.

Lana heard all the neighbors' voices.

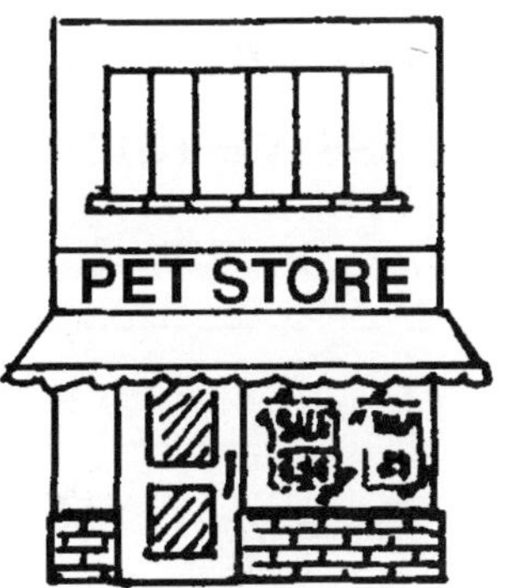

Practice

✎ Complete each sentence. Change the noun in ( ) to the correct singular or plural possessive form. Write it in the blank.

1. The pet ________________ sounds were confusing. (shop)
2. The two ________________ words were OATS and WATER. (bowls)
3. Lana's new ________________ name was Smith. (family)
4. The ________________ tunnel let Lana go from one side of her cage to the other. (wall)
5. The ______________ soft sounds made Lana feel safe. (voices)
6. ________________ busy activity amazed Cara. (Lana)

Name ______________________________ Date ______________

A Noun's Noun

☞ Form the possessive of a singular noun by adding an apostrophe and *s*.

pet—pet's girl—girl's

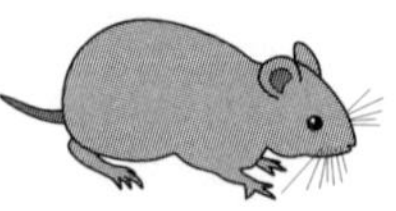

☞ Form the possessive of a plural noun that ends in *s* by adding an apostrophe only.

animal—animals' parents—parents'

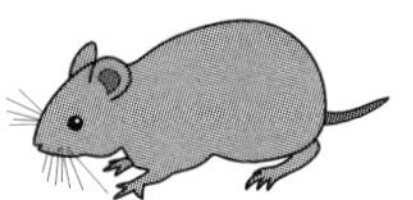

Practice

✎ Complete each sentence. Write the possessive form of the noun in ( ) in the blank.

1. The ______________ wish was to have a pet. (child)
2. Her ______________ pets were so much fun! (friends)
3. One day she went in her ______________ car to the pet shop. (dad)
4. There were rabbits in the ______________ window. (shop)
5. The girl went right over to the ______________ cages. (hamsters)
6. One ______________ face was really cute. (animal)
7. The ______________ eyes seemed to follow the girl. (creature)
8. The ______________ newest member was Lana. (family)
9. ______________ gift for Lana was a new cage. (Father)
10. The ______________ walls were made of plastic. (cage)

Name ______________________________ Date ______________

Go Verbs!

☞ An **action verb** is a word that shows an action. It is found in the predicate of a sentence.

Emma <u>zoomed</u> down the track.

Jimmy <u>dares</u> her to try the train track.

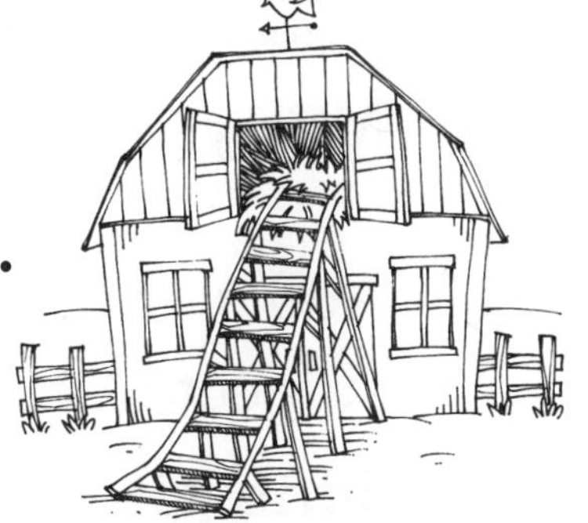

Practice

✎ Complete each sentence.
Choose an action verb from the box and write it in the blank.

flipped	brushed	made	zoomed	thought
added	squeezed	shouted	hit	tested
started	said	raced	dashed	stopped

1. Two girls ______________ a homemade train.
2. The track for the train ______________ at the hayloft window.
3. Emma ______________ the track to be sure it was steady.
4. She ______________ herself into the tiny train car.
5. Then the car ______________ down the track.
6. Emma ______________ , "I'm flying!"
7. The car ______________ the ground so hard that it ______________ over.
8. Emma ______________ the dirt off her clothes.
9. Emma ______________ about how to make the train track work better.
10. The girls ______________ more boards to the track.
11. Emma ______________ down again.
12. The car ______________ at the bottom of the track.

Name ______________________________ Date ______________

Now and Then

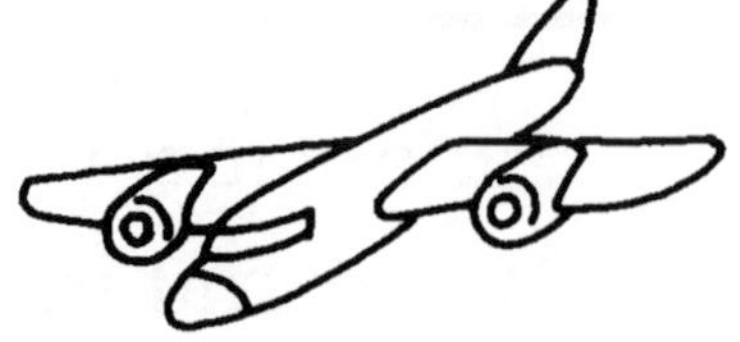

☞ **Present tense verbs** tell about actions that are happening now.

Many women <u>fly</u> planes today.

☞ Add *s* or *es* to most present tense verbs when the subject of the sentence tells about one thing.

This pilot <u>reads</u> about Amelia Earhart's adventures.

☞ **Past tense verbs** tell about actions in the past. To form the past tense of many action verbs, add *ed* to most present tense verbs.

Amelia always <u>wanted</u> to learn to fly.

Practice

✏ Complete each sentence. Use the present tense or past tense verb in ( ). Write the word in the blank.

1. Amelia Earhart was the first woman pilot who ______________ the Atlantic Ocean alone. (cross—past)
2. Once Amelia ______________ the White House. (visit—past)
3. Amelia never ______________ her trip around the world. (finish—past)
4. Today one of her planes ______________ in a museum in Washington, D.C. (hang—present)
5. No one ______________ what happened to Amelia. (know—present)
6. Many people ______________ for her. (wait—past)

Name ______________________________ Date ______________

It Happened Then

☞ To form the past tense of many verbs that end with *e*, drop the *e* and add *ed*.

carve—carved live—lived

☞ To form the past tense of one-syllable verbs that end with a vowel and a consonant, double the final consonant. Then add *ed*.

step—stepped drag—dragged

☞ To form the past tense of verbs that end in a consonant and *y*, change the *y* to *i*. Then add *ed*.

carry—carried empty—emptied

Practice

✏ Complete each sentence with the past tense form of the verb in ( ).

1. The river ______________ the land in new ways. (shape)
2. The river ______________ as it cut its way through the mountains. (hum)
3. As time went on, settlers ___________ along its banks. (move)
4. These people _______ to build new lives for themselves. (try)
5. The river ______________ their lives. (change)
6. The people ______________ new ways to do things. (plan)
7. People ______________ to build farms and towns. (hurry)
8. The settlers _________ the river for many things. (use)
9. It ________________ them with many of their needs. (supply)
10. The river has never ________________ flowing. (stop)

Name ______________________________ Date ________________

I Am a Linking Verb

☞ A **linking verb** connects the subject with words in the predicate. It tells what the subject is or is like.

The man <u>was</u> lonely.

That girl <u>is</u> a kind and loyal princess.

☞ The following forms of *be* are often used as linking verbs.

Verb	Present	Past	Past with *Have, Has,* or *Had*
be	am, is, are	was, were	been

Practice

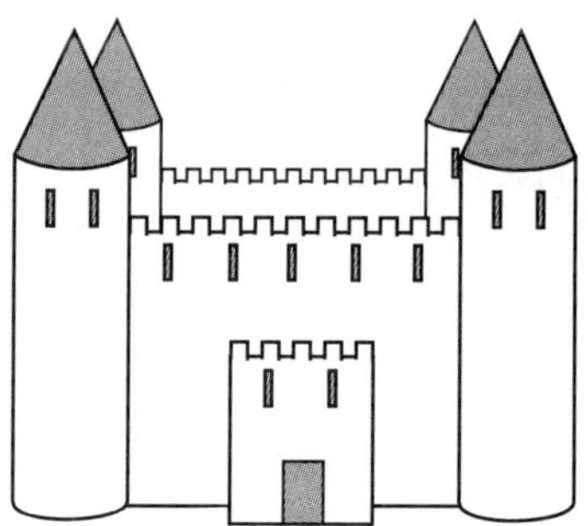

✎ Complete each sentence. Choose and circle the correct form of the verb in ( ).

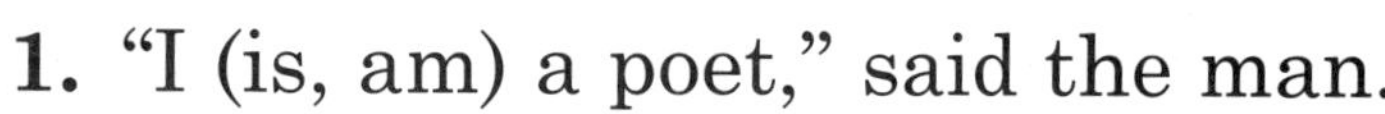

1. "I (is, am) a poet," said the man.
2. The girl thought his poems (was, were) beautiful.
3. Some people in the kingdom (is, are) evil.
4. The king (was, were) helpless.
5. The girl (was, were) a loving daughter.
6. The words (was, were) different in the man's poem.
7. The new poem (was, were) helpful to the king.
8. Thanks to the poet, the people (is, are) free.
9. "I (is, am) grateful to you," said the king to the poet.

Name ______________________________ Date ______________

Help Me, Verb!

☞ Sometimes a verb is made up of two or more words. The **main verb** tells about the action.

☞ A **helping verb** helps the main verb tell about an action.

The wind <u>has done</u> some strange things.

Windstorms <u>have moved</u> bodies of water.

☞ The following words are often used as helping verbs.

am	is	are	was	were	can	have	has	had	will

Practice

✐ Complete each sentence. Choose and circle the correct helping verb in ( ).

1. People (has, have) used wind power for many years.
2. Wind (has, have) moved boats and windmills.
3. A glider (can, has) float on the wind.
4. People (has, have) built sailboats.
5. Winds also (can, have) carry balloons.
6. The wind (can, has) blow clouds quickly.
7. Winds (can, are) push many things.
8. Strong winds (can, have) formed tornadoes.
9. Some tornadoes (has, have) winds of over a hundred miles an hour.
10. Sometimes the wind (has, have) harmed people.
11. Windy storms (have, can) moved trucks.
12. Wind power (has, have) made windmills work, too.

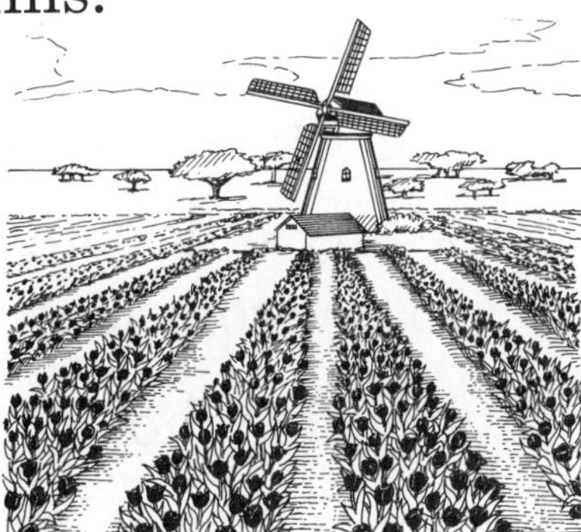

Name ______________________________ Date ______________

The Cat Came Back

☞ The verb *come* shows present and past in unusual ways.

This cat always comes back.

Why do you think she came back all the time?

Now that the cat has come back, what will they do?

The people have come to the end of their patience!

☞ These are the different forms of *come*.

Verb	Present	Past	Past with *Have, Has,* or *Had*
come	come(s)	came	come

Practice

✎ Complete each sentence. Use the correct form of the verb *come*. Write it in the blank.

1. Have you ______________ across other folk songs in books? (past with *have*)
2. Many folk songs ______________ down to us from long ago. (past)
3. People who ______________ from other countries brought many songs with them. (past)
4. This song is about a cat that always ______________ back. (present)
5. Did you know a cat who ______________ back all the time? (past)
6. Where had this cat ______________ from? (past with *had*)

Name ______________________________ Date ______________

It's a Go!

☞ The verb *go* shows present and past in unusual ways.

The kite and rope go upward to the tower.

The emperor goes on wings.

The other children went away.

The evil men have gone to prison.

☞ These are the different forms of *go*.

Verb	Present	Past	Past with *Have, Has*, or *Had*
go	go(es)	went	gone

Practice

✎ Complete each sentence. Use the correct form of the verb *go*.

1. Venessa used to ________ to play with her kite.
2. A carriage ________ past the palace every day.
3. The emperor had ________ to a grand party.
4. Venessa ________ to the party, too.
5. From the beginning she had ________ to see her father every day.
6. Earlier, Venessa ________ to her father with the cake.
7. Now the emperor has ________ to blow out the candles.
8. Then, Venessa and the emperor ________ back to the palace.

Name ______________________ Date ____________

Not Your Average Verb

☞ **Irregular verbs** are verbs that do not add *ed* to show past tense.

The bear was sorry he <u>met</u> the hunter.

The campers <u>have given</u> their leader a nickname.

☞ Some of these irregular verbs are in the chart.

Verb	Present	Past	Past with *Have, Has,* or *Had*
keep	keep(s)	kept	kept
sing	sing(s)	sang	sung
give	give(s)	gave	given
begin	begin(s)	began	begun
say	say(s)	said	said
think	think(s)	thought	thought

Practice

✏ Complete each sentence. Choose and circle the correct form of the verb in ( ).

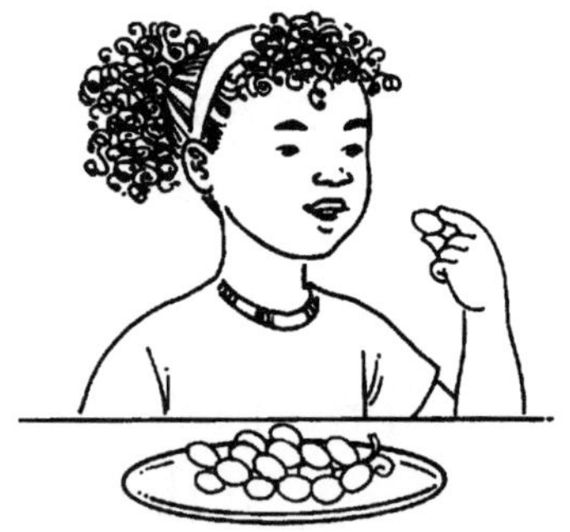

1. Elsa had (begin, begun) to eat toasted marshmallows long before dinner.
2. Some people (sing, sung) songs at camp.
3. Isabel (keep, kept) on eating the marshmallows, too.
4. Isabel (say, says) that marshmallows are delicious.
5. Elsa probably has (think, thought) so, too.
6. Too many marshmallows have (gave, given) the girls stomachaches.

Name ______________________ Date ____________

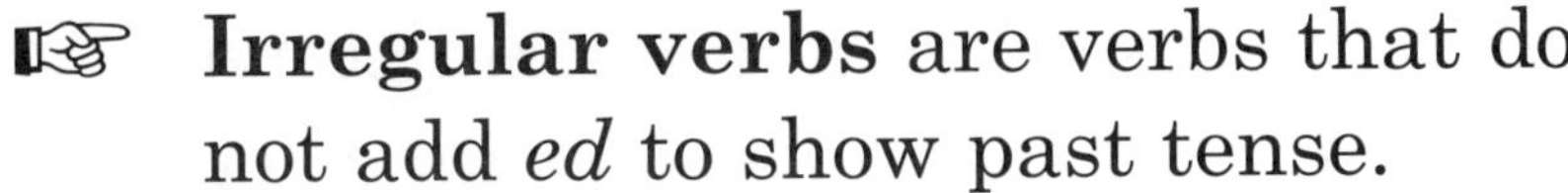

More Irregular Verbs

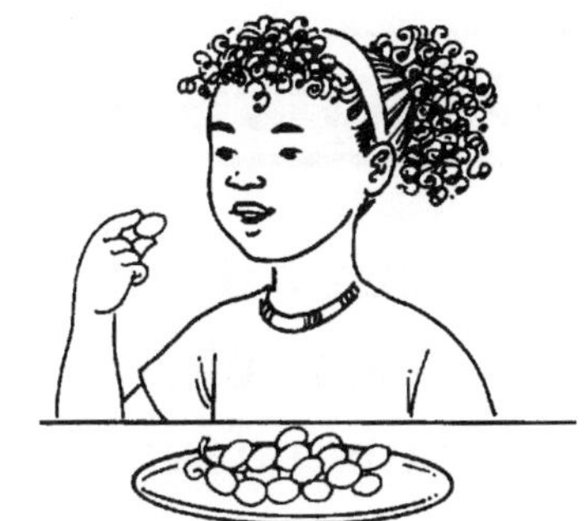

☞ **Irregular verbs** are verbs that do not add *ed* to show past tense.

☞ Some of these verbs are in the chart.

Verb	Present	Past	Past with *Have, Has*, or *Had*
eat	eat(s)	ate	eaten
run	run(s)	ran	run
take	take(s)	took	taken
meet	meet(s)	met	met
ring	ring(s)	rang	rung
keep	keep(s)	kept	kept
say	say(s)	said	said

✏ Complete each sentence. Use the correct form of the verb in ( ).

1. The bell has ____________ for dinner. (ring—past with *has*)
2. You could say that she really ____________ the cake. (take—past)
3. She could have ____________ she had eaten enough. (say—past with *have*)
4. Is there a marshmallow she did not ________ ? (eat—present)
5. It would not matter to Elsa if the camp __________ out of food. (run—past)
6. Elsa is so full of marshmallows that she ____________ saying she will never eat again! (keep—present)
7. I have never ____________ a girl like Elsa. (meet—past)

Name ______________________ Date ____________

Describe It!

☞ An **adjective** is a word that describes a noun. Adjectives can tell *how many, what color,* or *what size or shape*. They also describe how something *feels, sounds, tastes,* or *smells*.

There must be a million ladybugs in the field.

The bees made a loud buzzing sound.

☞ *A, an,* and *the* are adjectives called **articles**. Use *a* before a singular noun that begins with a consonant sound. Use *an* before a singular noun that begins with a vowel sound.

The girls were in an alfalfa field.

I like the color you see on a lizard's belly.

Practice

✎ Complete each sentence. Add an *adjective* (adj.) or an *article* to each. Use the adjectives in the box.

reddish	soft	many	hundred
a	the	white	

1. The girls saw a ____________ bugs. (adj.—how many)
2. They lay down on ____________ grass. (adj.—feel)
3. I named ____________ things I like. (adj.—how many)
4. Her favorite color is ____________ brown. (adj.—what color)
5. I thought ____________ morning air was the best. (article)
6. ____________ ladybug tickled my nose. (article)
7. I watched the ____________ clouds. (adj.—what color)

Name ______________________________ Date ______________

Good, Better, Best

☞ Add *er* to most one-syllable adjectives when they are used to compare two things.

Winter days are <u>shorter</u> than summer days.

☞ Add *est* to most one-syllable adjectives when they are used to compare more than two things.

Caribou make the <u>longest</u> migrations of all land animals.

☞ The word *more* may be used to compare two things. Use *more* with many adjectives of two syllables. Use *more* with adjectives of three or more syllables.

It is <u>more difficult</u> to find food in the winter than in the summer.

☞ The word *most* may be used to compare more than two things. Use *most* with many adjectives of two syllables. Use *most* with adjectives of three or more syllables.

The gray whale makes the <u>most amazing</u> migration of all.

Practice

✎ Complete each sentence. Use the correct form of the adjective in ( ).

1. As summer ends, the weather gets ____________. (cool)
2. Many animals make the ________ trips of their lives. (hard)
3. Migrating is the ________ ____________________ thing that many animals do. (important)
4. It is ________ ____________________ to live in a warm climate than in a cold one. (comfortable)

Name ______________________ Date ______________

Compare!

☞ Add *er* to most adjectives that compare two things.

short—shorter **cool—cooler**

☞ Add *est* to most adjectives that compare three or more things.

warm—warmest **long—longest**

☞ If an adjective ends with one vowel letter and one consonant, double the consonant before adding *er* or *est*.

hot—hotter **big—biggest**

☞ When an adjective ends with *e*, drop the *e* before adding *er* or *est*.

brave—braver **large—largest**

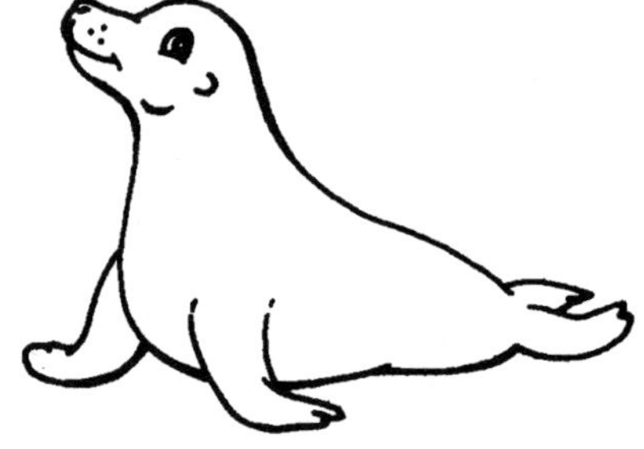

Practice

✎ Complete each sentence with the correct form of the adjective in ( ).

1. Caribou are ____________ than seals. (large)
2. Their winter fur is ______________ than their summer fur. (thick)
3. The mother seal is _______________ than the baby seal. (thin)
4. The baby seal is the _______________baby mammal of all. (cute)
5. The whale is the _______________ of all animals. (strong)

Name ______________________ Date ______________

In Place of a Noun

☞ A **pronoun** is a word that takes the place of one or more nouns.

Ruby Rabbit was delighted.

She thought the hutch was a great home.

Neighbors dropped by.

They had kind, friendly voices.

☞ A **singular pronoun** names one person, place, or thing. The words *I, me, you, he, she, him, her,* and *it* are singular pronouns.

A name had been chosen for Ruby Rabbit.

It would be painted on the hutch.

☞ A **plural pronoun** names more than one person, place, or thing. The words *we, you, they, us,* and *them* are plural pronouns.

Grown-ups did not believe Karen.

They just do not understand these things.

Practice

Read each sentence. Think of a pronoun to use in place of the underlined word or words. Write the pronoun in the blank.

1. The hutch was divided into two rooms. ______________
2. Daddy will paint the name. ______________
3. Mother did not see Ruby's name. ______________
4. The girl liked Ruby's name. ______________
5. The neighbors stared at Ruby. ______________
6. My friends and I will call you Ruby. ______________
7. Ruby was tired and happy. ______________

Name ______________________ Date ______________

These Nouns Are Pros

☞ These pronouns are used in the subject of a sentence.

Singular	Plural
I	we
you	you
he, she, it	they

"I will build a big pit," said the lion.

☞ These pronouns follow action verbs.

Singular	Plural
me	us
you	you
him, her, it	them

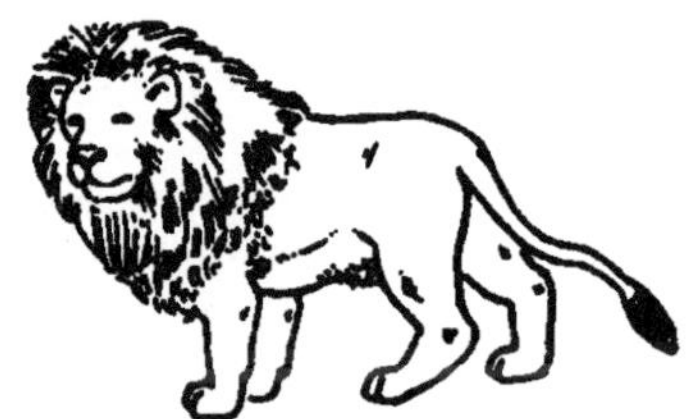

The lioness invited <u>them</u> to the party.

Practice

Read each pair of sentences. Then complete the second sentence in each pair. Write a pronoun in place of the underlined word or words.

1. <u>The lion and lioness</u> were very hungry. _______ needed meat to eat.
2. <u>The lion</u> thought for a while. Then _______ had an idea.
3. <u>The lioness and I</u> will have a party. _______ will invite the neighbors.
4. Mr. Dog told <u>his wife</u> about the party. Mr. Dog did not want _______ to go.
5. <u>The dog and the goat</u> tricked the lion. _______ did not go to the party.

Name ______________________________ Date ______________

Working Together

☞ A **compound word** is formed by putting together two smaller words.

blackberry	**treetop**	**sunlight**	**inside**

Practice

✎ **A.** Add a word from Box 1 to a word from Box 2. Say the compound words.

Box 1		
tree	after	flash
lady	dog	school
some	under	country

Box 2		
bug	house	noon
day	tops	side
light	ground	teacher

✎ **B.** The second part of a compound word is in ( ). Think of what the first part should be. Write the compound word in the blank.

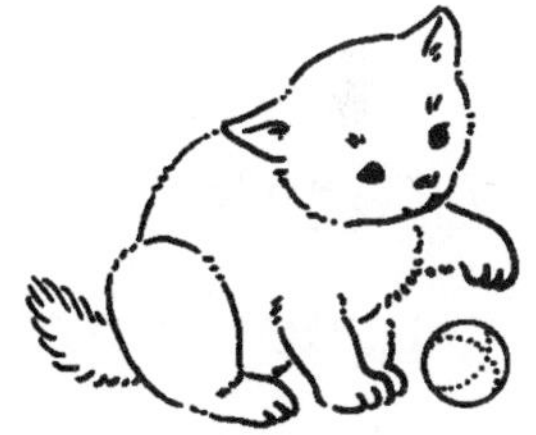

1. Jenny ____________ fed the lost kitten. (self)
2. The kitten could not find food for ____________ . (self)
3. The kitten's bed was kept ____________ . (side)
4. Does the dog live in the ______________________ ? (house)
5. Jenny left her _________________ to visit the kitten. (room)
6. The kitten hid in the __________________________ . (noon)
7. Do spiders live ______________________________ ? (ground)

Name ______________________________ Date ______________

Short Cuts

☞ A **contraction** is a short way of writing two words together. Some of the letters are left out. An apostrophe (') takes their place.

is + not = isn't	**I + am = I'm**
are + not = aren't	**you + are = you're**
have + not = haven't	**she + is = she's**
was + not = wasn't	**it + is = it's**
were + not = weren't	**we + are = we're**
had + not = hadn't	**they + are = they're**

Practice

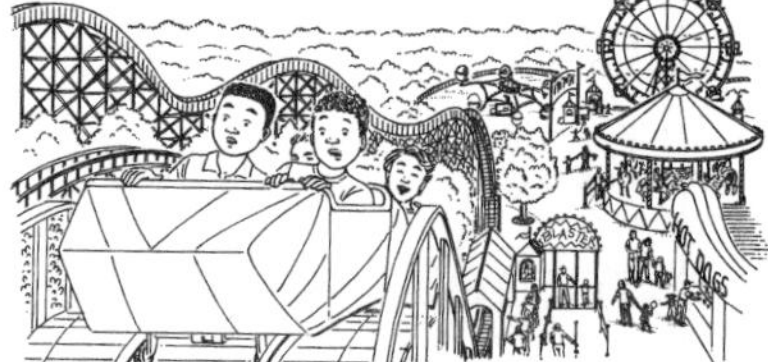

✎ Read the sentence. Write a contraction for each underlined set of words in the blank.

1. Lucy had not been on a roller coaster before. ______________
2. She thinks they are much too fast. ______________
3. Katherine has not been on one in years. ______________
4. She is going to the amusement park! ______________
5. You are riding on a great roller coaster. ______________
6. I am not going to ride it. ______________
7. You have not tried it yet. ______________
8. It is the largest one in the state. ______________
9. Lucy and Jimmy were not at the gate. ______________
10. The ride was not long enough. ______________
11. The world's tallest roller coaster is not in the United States.

    ____
12. It is in the country of Japan. ______________
13. We are not ready to try it out. ______________

Name ______________________ Date ______________

Unit Two Assessment: Sentences

Finish the sentences. Add a subject or a predicate of your own to make a complete sentence.

1. My family ______________________.
2. ______________________ likes to dig holes in the yard.

Write whether each question is telling, asking, a command, or an exclamation.

3. The stove is hot! ______________________
4. How long has it been on? ______________________
5. It has been on all day. ______________________
6. Don't touch it. ______________________

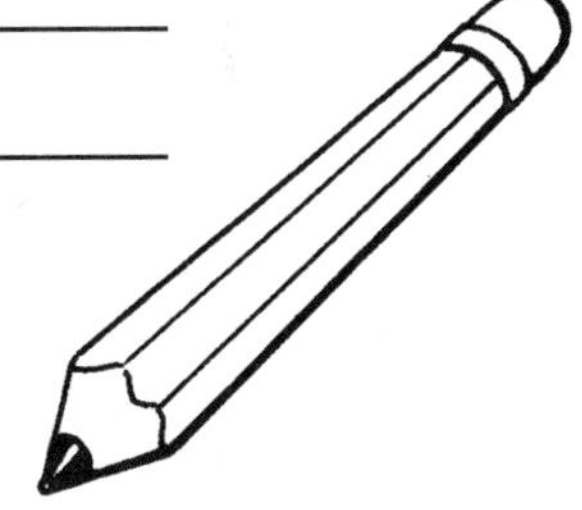

Combine the sentences to make one sentence.

7. Robins sing a pretty song. Cardinals sing a pretty song.
____
8. Bears hibernate in the winter. Bears stay warm in the winter. ______________________
9. We were looking for a book. My sister found it for me.
____
____
10. The flowers are bright. The flowers are pretty. The flowers are colorful. ______________________

Add an adjective to make the sentence more interesting.

11. The ______________________ horse ran through the grass.

Name ______________________________ Date ______________

What's in a Sentence?

☞ A **sentence** is a group of words that tells a complete thought. Every sentence begins with a capital letter.

Manny thought that Tony had pinched him.

This made Tony angry.

☞ Every sentence has two parts. The **subject** of a sentence is the part about which something is being said.

<u>The two friends</u> sat very still.

<u>The crab</u> thought they looked very funny.

☞ The **predicate** is all the words that tell something about the subject.

Manny and Tony <u>found out who pinched them</u>.

They <u>wanted to remain good friends</u>.

Practice

Finish the sentences. Add a subject or a predicate of your own to make each group a complete sentence.

1. Manny and Tony ______________________________.
2. The warm sun ______________________________.
3. ______________________ jumped when he was pinched.
4. ______________________ did not like being called a name.
5. Soon Tony ______________________________.
6. A little red lump ______________________________.
7. For a long time the friends ______________________.
8. ______________________ giggled and ran away.

Name ______________________ Date ______________

Telling or Asking

☞ A **statement** tells something. It ends with a period (.).

The crab was the real pincher.

He laughed and ran away.

☞ A **question** asks something. It ends with a question mark (?).

Will Manny and Tony find out the truth?

Where will they swim now?

Practice

Read each sentence. Decide if each sentence is a *statement* or a *question*. Then add the correct punctuation mark at the end of each sentence.

1. Why did the crab laugh at Manny and Tony
2. Maybe he pinched them to make them mad at each other
3. Would you like to be friends with a crab
4. Someone who pinches is not a good friend
5. Did you think Tony pinched Manny
6. Tony would not hurt Manny
7. Where did the crab hide
8. Manny and Tony know the meaning of friendship
9. They know that friends should not pinch each other
10. The friends settled their argument in a smart way
11. Will they trust each other from now on
12. Manny and Tony went to the beach the next day

Name ______________________________ Date ______________

Command and Exclaim

☞ A **command** gives an order or a direction. It ends with a period (.).

You have to catch a hundred flies.

Put the flies in a jar.

☞ An **exclamation** shows strong feeling. It ends with an exclamation point (!).

I cannot believe wolf spiders have eight eyes!

They run so fast!

Practice

✎ Read each sentence. Decide if each sentence is a *command* or an *exclamation*. Then add the correct punctuation mark at the end of each sentence.

1. Flies are really hard to catch
2. Get ready to put the fly in the jar
3. Stay away from the spider
4. You can really catch flies
5. I do not want a spider in this house
6. Bring the spider to the pet store
7. Be sure to give the spider water to drink
8. Put the spider in a box with a wire screen over the top
9. The spider runs fast
10. Tell us what to do
11. Feed the spider today
12. The spider escaped

Name ________________________________ Date ______________

Putting Them Together

☞ A good writer sometimes **combines**, or joins, sentence parts. The word *and* is often used to combine sentence parts.

☞ When two sentences have the same predicate, the subject can often be combined.

Fall brings changes.

Winter brings changes.

Fall and winter bring changes.

How to Combine Subjects

1. Write the two subjects. Use the word *and* between them. Finish the sentence with the predicate.
2. Be sure to use the correct form of the verb.

Practice

✎ Combine the subjects of these sentences. Use the word *and*. Write the new sentences.

1. Robins sing in spring. Cardinals sing in spring.

____

2. Animals awake from a long winter's sleep.
Insects awake from a long winter's sleep.

____

3. The animals are active in summer.
The birds are active in summer.

____

4. Snakes hibernate in winter. Toads hibernate in winter.

____

Name ______________________________ Date ______________

A Good Combination

☞ A good writer sometimes **combines**, or joins, sentence parts. The word *and* is often used to combine them.

☞ When two sentences have the same subject, the predicates may be combined.

Daniel wanted a book. Daniel went to find one.

Daniel wanted a book and went to find one.

How to Combine Predicates

1. Look for sentences that have the same subject. If the sentences are short, you may be able to combine the predicates.
2. Write the subject. Then write the two predicates. Use the word *and* between the predicates.

Practice

✎ Combine the predicates of these sentences.
Use the word *and*. Write the new sentences.

1. Daniel mounted his scooter. Daniel went to the library.

   ____

2. The librarian saw Daniel.

   The librarian asked if he needed help.

   ____

3. Daniel took the book. Daniel checked it out.

   ____

4. Mama stopped cooking.

   Mama looked at the book Daniel had gotten.

   ____

Name ______________________________ Date ______________

Combine and Describe

☞ To avoid choppy sentences, a writer may combine adjectives. The adjectives should describe the same subject.

The field of alfalfa is soft.

The field of alfalfa is green.

The field of alfalfa is quiet.

The field of alfalfa is soft, green, and quiet.

How to Combine Sentences with Adjectives
1. Look for different adjectives that describe the same subject.
2. Use *and* to combine them.
3. Use commas to separate three or more adjectives in a row.

Practice

✎ Combine each set of sentences into one sentence. Use the word *and*. Write the new sentences.

1. The rocky cliffs are steep.
The rocky cliffs are bare.

____

2. The summer sky is clear. The summer sky is blue.
The summer sky is beautiful.

____

3. The flowers in the field are pretty. The flowers in the field are yellow. The flowers in the field are tall.

____

4. The alfalfa smells sweet.
The alfalfa smells fresh.

____

Name ________________________________ Date ______________

Smooth It Out

☞ A writer can join two short, choppy sentences with the word *and*.

The river rushed through the land.

It cut through mountains.

The river rushed through the land, <u>and</u> it cut through the mountains.

How to Combine Sentences with *and*
1. Find two sentences that tell about the same thing.
2. Use the word *and* to join them.
3. Put a comma before the word *and*.

Practice

✎ Combine each pair of sentences.
Use the word *and*. Write the new sentences.

1. Explorers followed rivers. They used the rivers like roads.

   ____

2. Loggers cut down trees. The trees floated down the river.

   ____

3. Indians used clay for pottery. Sometimes they used clay for bricks.

   ____

4. The river is beautiful. It is also useful.

   ____

5. Settlers looked for the right place. They built new homes.

   ____

6. More and more people settled in America. The river towns grew.

   ____

Name ______________________________ Date ______________

Make It Clear

☞ A good writer uses **exact verbs**. Exact verbs clearly describe an action. They make sentences more interesting to read.

My daughter <u>turns</u> straw into gold.

My daughter <u>spins</u> straw into gold.

The king <u>asked</u> to meet the daughter.

The king <u>demanded</u> to meet the daughter.

How to Write Sentences with Exact Verbs

1. Think carefully about the actions of your subject.
2. List interesting verbs that describe each action clearly.
3. Choose the clearest verb for each action.
4. Write each sentence, using the clearest verb.

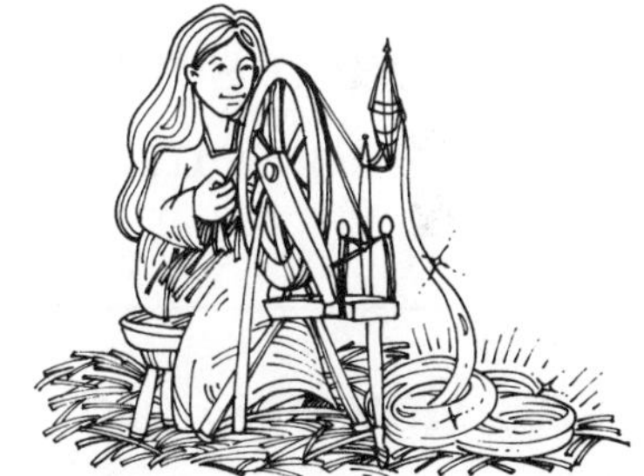

Practice

✎ Write each sentence. Replace each underlined verb with an exact verb. Write your new verb on the line.

1. The miller <u>talked</u> __________________ about his daughter.
2. Rumpelstiltskin <u>fooled</u> __________________ the daughter.
3. The king <u>wanted</u> __________________ more gold.
4. Rumpelstiltskin <u>moved</u> __________________ to the straw.
5. The messenger <u>looked</u> __________________ for different names.
6. Rumpelstiltskin <u>walked</u> __________________ around the fire.
7. The queen <u>said</u> __________________ different names.

Name ______________________ Date ______________

Clearly Better

☞ A writer can make short sentences clearer by adding adjectives that give exact **details**.

I walked through the field.

I walked through the alfalfa field.

How to Add Details to Sentences

1. Look for sentences that do not give a clear enough picture of your idea.
2. Think of adjectives that give a more exact picture. Think of how something looks, sounds, tastes, smells, or feels.
3. Choose the adjectives that explain your idea most clearly.
4. Add these words to your sentences.

Practice

✎ Read each sentence. Add adjectives to make each sentence more interesting to read.

1. The ______________ field looked like a ______________ carpet.
2. The flowers had a ______________ smell.
3. Ladybugs crawled on my ______________ jeans.
4. Clouds floated across the ______________ sky.
5. I like the ______________ sound of the wind.
6. The ______________ sun felt good on my face.
7. The ______________ sound of bees filled the air.
8. I like the ______________ rain.
9. Mother makes ______________ bread.

Name ______________________ Date ______________

Perfectly Clear

☞ A good writer begins sentences in different ways. Sometimes a writer begins sentences with words that tell *when.*

I read about spiders <u>today</u>.

<u>Today</u> I read about spiders.

How to Change Sentence Beginnings

1. Find some sentences that begin with the same word.
2. See if any of these sentences tell *when.*
3. Move the word or words that tell *when* to the beginning of the sentence.

Practice

Find the word or words in each sentence that tell *when.* Then write each sentence in a different way. Begin with the word or words that tell *when.*

1. We read about spiders in class today.

   ____

2. I had read about spiders last year.

   ____

3. The teacher then showed pictures of spiders.

   ____

4. Some spiders spin webs at night.

   ____

5. I saw a spider in the garden yesterday.

   ____

6. I will bring my spider poster tomorrow.

   ____

Name ______________________________ Date ______________

Unit Three Assessment: Vocabulary and Usage

Circle the word that is a synonym for the first word in each group.

1. large	small	big	tiny
2. hunted	searched	climbed	worked
3. like	fear	ignore	enjoy

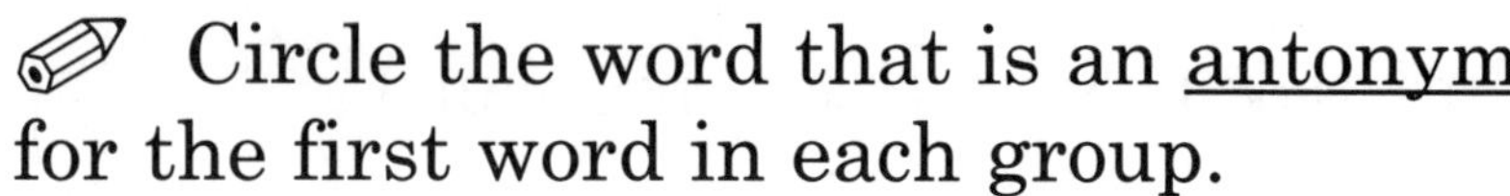

Circle the word that is an antonym for the first word in each group.

4. always	usually	never	often
5. laughed	cried	giggled	snored
6. simple	easy	lost	hard

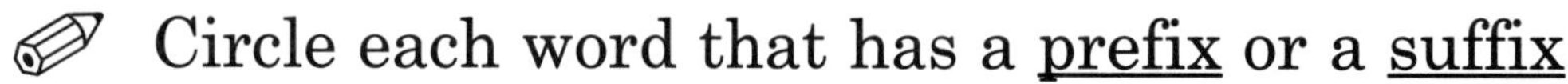

Circle each word that has a prefix or a suffix.

7. dislike	**10.** impossible	**13.** redo
8. unlucky	**11.** reappear	**14.** luck
9. taste	**12.** patiently	**15.** hopeful

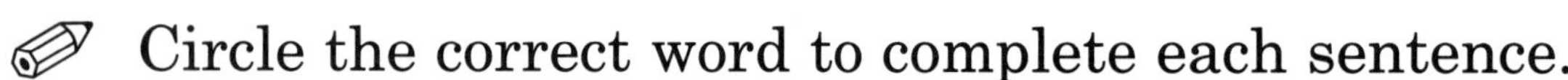

Circle the correct word to complete each sentence.

16. There are (two, too) people in the boat.

17. He had a tear in his (I, eye).

18. They just (ate, eight) dinner.

19. When (I, me) grow up, I want to be a dancer.

20. Will you show (I, me) the way?

21. We (enjoy, enjoys) eating spaghetti.

22. She (look, looks) like my sister.

Name ______________________________ Date ______________

Like Meanings

☞ A **synonym** is a word that has almost the same meaning as another word. Here are some synonyms for the word *empty*.

empty	bare, blank, hollow, open

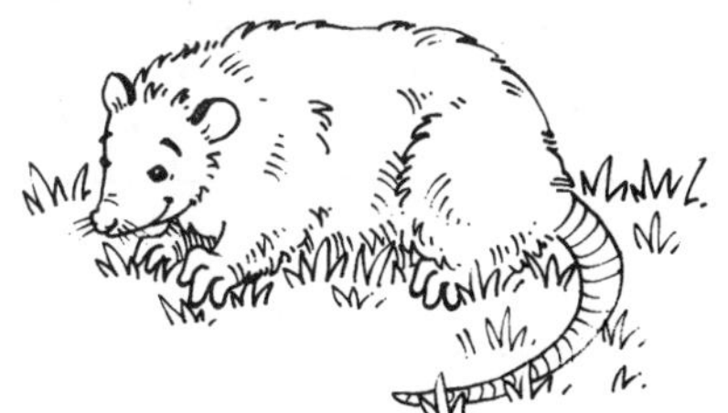

Practice

✎ Read each sentence. Choose a synonym in ( ) for the underlined word. Circle your choice.

1. People made the little animals feel <u>afraid</u>. (happy, excited, scared)
2. Whenever he saw them, he was very <u>still</u>. (fast, quiet, hungry)
3. Sometimes he heard people <u>approaching</u> near him. (coming, eating, working)
4. He would <u>tremble</u> at the sight of them. (shake, laugh, dig)
5. Once some people <u>found</u> him lying in the grass. (discovered, heard, lost)
6. He had <u>hunted</u> for food but had found none. (worked, climbed, searched)
7. Food was <u>hard</u> to find. (difficult, easy, simple)
8. The people <u>rescued</u> him by giving him food. (saved, left, thanked)
9. He <u>started</u> a new life with them. (ended, began, liked)
10. The possum <u>liked</u> his new friends. (enjoyed, feared, ignored)

Name ______________________________ Date ______________

Opposite Meanings

☞ An **antonym** is a word that means the opposite of another word. Here are some antonyms for the word *big*.

big	small, tiny, little, slight

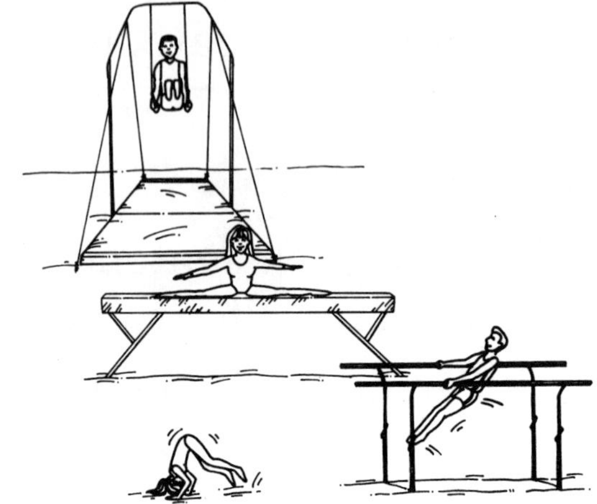

Practice

✎ Read each sentence. Choose an antonym from the box to replace the underlined word in each sentence. Write your choice on the line.

true	fast	started	ended	cried	never
under	easy	before	always	something	hard

1. Donna <u>stopped</u> taking gymnastics classes. ______________
2. Donna found that gymnastics was <u>easy</u>. ______________
3. It is <u>false</u> that she was a poor gymnast. ______________
4. She <u>never</u> practiced at home. ______________
5. Donna <u>laughed</u> when she tripped. ______________
6. <u>After</u> Donna fell, she liked gymnastics. ______________
7. Now Donna has <u>started</u> her gymnastics classes. ______________
8. Earl and Ralph <u>always</u> worked. ______________
9. They hid <u>over</u> the tree and watched. ______________
10. Donna tried <u>nothing</u> else. ______________
11. It was <u>difficult</u> to make a carving. ______________
12. Donna was a <u>slow</u> runner. ______________

Name ______________________________ Date ______________

Before the Word...

☞ A **prefix** is a letter or group of letters added to the beginning of a base word. A prefix changes the meaning of a word.

I agree that the pet needs a name.

I disagree with your ideas for names.

Prefix	Meaning	Example
dis	not	dislike
im	not	impossible
re	again	redo
re	back	repay
un	not	unlucky
un	opposite of	unwrap

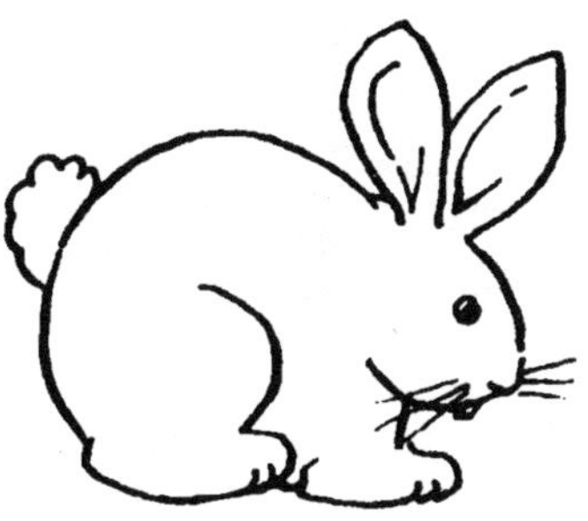

Practice

✏ Read each sentence. Change the meaning of each sentence by adding a prefix from the list above to each underlined word. Write the new word on the line.

1. Lexi was a very usual animal. ______________
2. She was patient to get out into the world. ______________
3. Lexi liked the pet store. ______________
4. Every night she felt lucky to be there. ______________
5. Lexi thought it was possible to find a new home. ______________
6. Her hutch was like the cage at the pet shop. ______________
7. Lexi traced her steps in the hutch. ______________
8. Julia came back and appeared at the door of Lexi's hutch. ______________

Name ______________________________ Date ______________

After the Word...

☞ A **suffix** is a letter or group of letters added to the ending of a base word. A suffix changes the meaning of a word.

Amelia made a roller coaster workable.

She was a very good thinker.

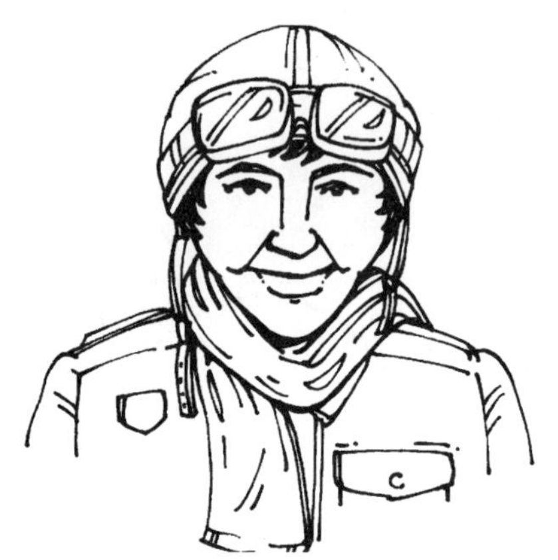

Suffix	**Meaning**	**Example**
able	able to be	wearable
er	one who	builder
ful	full of	hopeful
ible	able to be	flexible
less	without	careless
or	one who	visitor

Practice

✎ Read each sentence. Choose a suffix from the above list to write a single word that has the same meaning as the words in ( ). Write the new word on the line. The first one is done for you.

1. Amelia Earhart was a (person who flies planes). aviator
2. When she was a girl, she was the (person who invents) of a roller coaster. ______________
3. It was a (full of use) ride. ______________
4. Her sister Muriel was her (person who helps). ______________
5. Amelia was (without fear) and rode on it. ______________
6. She felt (full of joy) as she flew down. ______________
7. Her first (full of success) ride ended at her grandmother's feet. ______________
8. She did not think the roller coaster was (without harm).

____

Name ______________________________ Date ______________

Alike and Different!

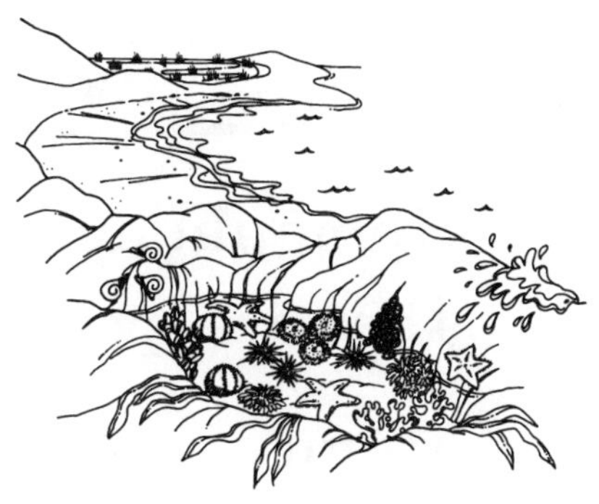

☞ **Homographs** are words that have the same spelling but different meanings.

felt—a soft kind of cloth

felt—sensed something on the skin

☞ Some homographs are pronounced differently.

wind—moving air

wind—to turn a knob on something, as a clock

Practice

✎ Write a new sentence with the homograph of the underlined word. Be sure you use a different meaning of the underlined word in your sentence. Use a dictionary if you need help.

1. Manny and Tony <u>will</u> be friends forever.

   ____

2. Tony likes to <u>lean</u> against a big rock.

   ____

3. Manny had a <u>wound</u> on his toe.

   ____

4. Manny will <u>lead</u> Tony to the tide pool.

   ____

5. Tony was pinched <u>last</u>.

   ____

6. Was there a <u>tear</u> on Manny's face?

   ____

7. Manny found a baseball <u>bat</u> on the beach.

   ____

Name ______________________ Date ______________

To, Too, or Two!

☞ **Homophones** are words that sound alike.
They are spelled differently and have different meanings.

Manny and Tony went <u>to</u> the beach.
What did the <u>two</u> friends see?

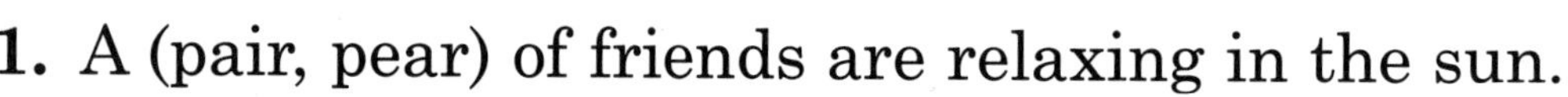

Practice

✎ Read each sentence. Choose and circle the correct homophone in ( ).

1. A (pair, pear) of friends are relaxing in the sun.
2. The (son, sun) is shining down on them.
3. Now (they're, there) having a fight.
4. Tony (knows, nose) Manny would not pinch.
5. Tony was (so, sew) angry.
6. (One, Won) toe turned red.
7. Manny could not (sea, see) another person.
8. (Their, There) was no one else on the beach.
9. They could only (here, hear) the ocean.
10. Finally, the friends (made, maid) up.
11. They were sorry (four, for) their mistake.
12. The crab is not (here, hear).
13. They left an (hour, our) later.
14. Manny (would, wood) believe Tony next time.
15. There was a tear in his (I, eye).
16. Manny and Tony looked at the deep (blue, blew) ocean.
17. Then they (ate, eight) some lunch.
18. Now they (know, no) who pinched them.

Name ______________________________ Date ______________

Abbreviate!

☞ An **abbreviation** is a short way of writing a word or words.

☞ These are abbreviations for titles of people.

Mr. **Ms.** **Mrs.** **Dr.**

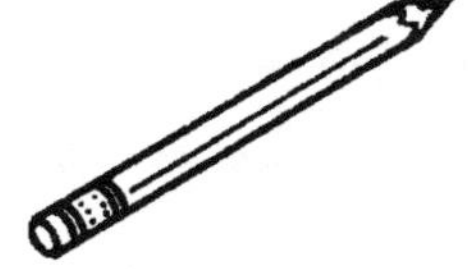

☞ Here are some common street abbreviations.

Street—St. **Avenue—Ave.** **Road—Rd.**

☞ There are abbreviations for days of the week and months of the year.

Monday—Mon. **Tuesday—Tues.** **Friday—Fri.**

January—Jan. **February—Feb.** **August—Aug.**

Practice

✏ Read each address and date. Write the underlined words as abbreviations.

1. 20 Encore Street ______________________
2. Chicago, Illinois 60018 ______________________
3. Monday, August 1 __________ __________
4. Mister Ed Schyler ______________________
5. 530 Remington Road ______________________
6. Lafayette, Indiana 47905 ______________________
7. Friday, February 22 __________ __________

Name ______________________________ Date ______________

Oh, Those Troublesome Words!

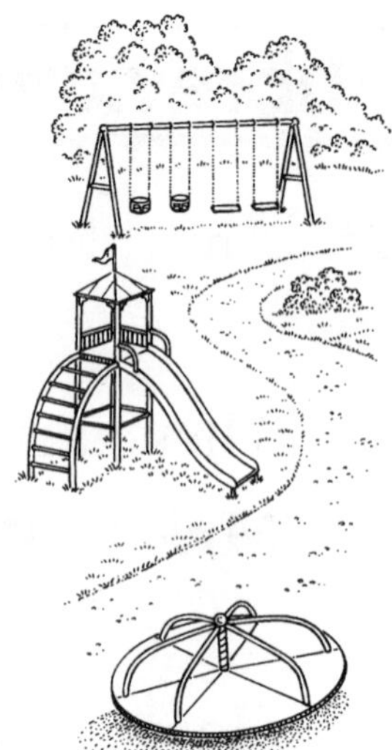

☞ Use *to* when you mean "in the direction of." Use *too* when you mean "also." Use *two* when you mean "one more than one."

> **Manny and Tony went *to* the beach.**
> **A crab was at the beach, *too*.**
> **The *two* friends did not see the crab.**

☞ Use *their* when you mean "belonging to them." Use *there* when you mean "in that place." Use *they're* when you mean "they are." *They're* is a contraction for *they are.*

> **They almost lost their friendship.**
> **The crab ran over there.**
> **They're going to be friends again.**

Practice

✎ Read each sentence. Choose and circle the correct word in ( ).

1. Let's go (too, to) the park.
2. We will see some other friends, (two, too).
3. I see (two, to) empty swings.
4. You ran (to, two) the swing I wanted.
5. (Too, Two) good friends should not argue.
6. Let's go (to, too) the beach instead.
7. (Their, There) is a good place to sit.
8. We will be close to the water over (there, they're).
9. The seagulls are looking for (there, their) lunch.
10. (They're, Their) heading for our lunch!
11. (Their, There) are some nice shells.
12. (They're, Their) just right for our sand castle.

Name ______________________ Date ______________

More Troublesome Words

☞ Use *your* when you mean "belonging to you." Use *you're* when you mean "you are." *You're* is a contraction for *you are*.

Your grandpa's story is amazing. **You're not going to believe it.**

☞ Use *its* when you mean "belonging to it." Use *it's* when you mean "it is." *It's* is a contraction for *it is*.

The wind blew with all its might. **It's the biggest wind there ever was!**

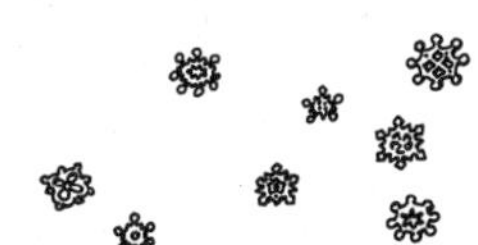

Practice

✏ Read each sentence. Choose and circle the correct word in ( ).

1. (Your, You're) new in this town.
2. Put (your, you're) suitcase here.
3. A big wind blew through (you're, your) town.
4. (Your, You're) going to think this tale is a big fib.
5. Did you lose (you're, your) cats and dogs?
6. Our house needed to have (it's, its) old roof fixed.
7. (Its, It's) just as well that we never fixed it.
8. Old Wind puffed out (its, it's) big fat cheeks.
9. (Its, It's) about to blow the roof off!
10. (It's, Its) what really happened!
11. Now (it's, its) raining cats and dogs!
12. I do not believe (your, you're) story.

Name ________________________ Date ____________

I and Me

☞ The word *I* is only used in the subject part of a sentence. The word *me* follows an action verb.

I have a story to tell you.
She and I enjoy listening to the story.
Tell me that old story again, Grandpa.

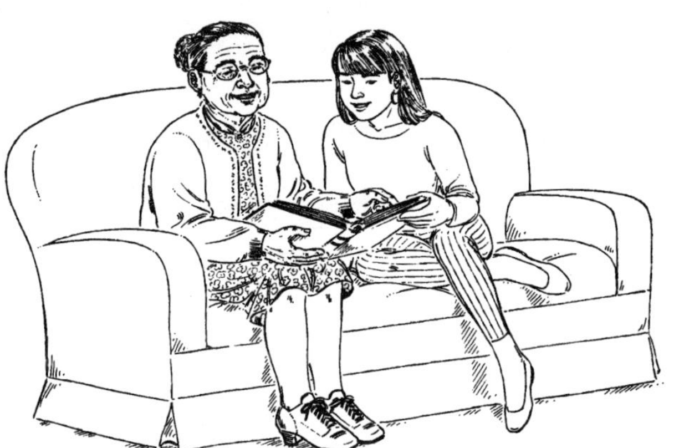

Practice

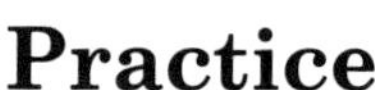 Read each sentence. Choose and circle the correct word in ( ).

1. (I, Me) love to look at my grandparents' old photograph album.
2. They tell (I, me) wonderful stories about the photos.
3. (Me, I) like to hear about my mother when she was my age.
4. She says she and (I, me) look so much alike.
5. Grandma and Grandpa say that (I, me) should know all about my family's history.
6. They tell (I, me) to remember the family's stories.
7. My brother, my sister, and (me, I) listen carefully.
8. When (me, I) grow up, I will tell my children the stories.
9. (Me, I) will show them the photograph album.
10. They will help (I, me) remember the stories.

Name ______________________________ Date ________________

Let's Agree

☞ To make most verbs agree with singular subjects, add *s*.

She walks along a sandy trail.

☞ To make verbs that end in *sh, ch, ss*, or *x* agree with singular subjects, add *es*.

The rain washes the flowers of the cacti.

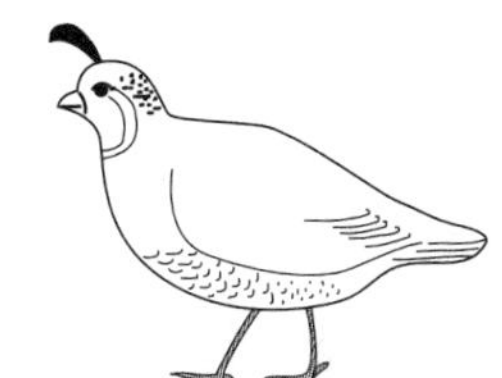

☞ To make most verbs agree with plural subjects, do not change the ending.

The birds sing after it rains.

Practice

✎ Read each sentence. Choose and circle the form of the verb that agrees with each subject.

1. The girl (stroll, strolls) with her grandmother.
2. The girl (watch, watches) everything around her.
3. She (enjoy, enjoys) the quail most.
4. Five quail (pass, passes) in front of her.
5. The girl (see, sees) quail eggs in a nest.
6. They (touch, touches) none of them.
7. Grandmother (take, takes) water from the cacti.
8. They (fill, fills) their basket with fruit.
9. Grandmother (teach, teaches) the girl about the desert.
10. The girl (understand, understands) how beautiful it is.

Name ______________________ Date ____________

Unit Four Assessment: Capitalization and Punctuation

Add the correct punctuation to each sentence. Use periods, question marks, exclamation points, commas, colons, apostrophes, underlines, and quotation marks.

1. "Where are you going?" asked Mrs Brown.
2. "I need to find my glasses," answered Mr Brown
3. We are going to be late if you dont hurry
4. We should arrive by 130 PM
5. Where did you see them last
6. They were on the book called The Old West.
7. There is a poem called The Old West, too.
8. Thats a fantastic poem
9. First we are going to Topeka Kansas.
10. The date was April 7 1995.

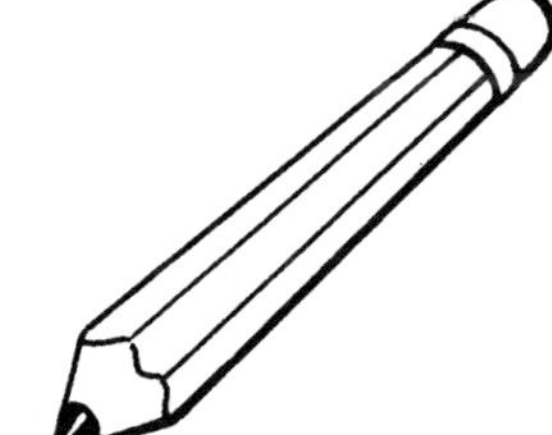

Write the sentences again using capital letters where they are needed.

11. my brother jimmy was born in washington on the fourth of july.

____

____

12. i live in the state of massachusetts in the united states.

____

____

13. barnaby is reading a book called in the saddle.

____

____

Name ______________________ Date ______________

Nutty Names

☞ Begin the first and last name of a person with a capital letter.

Penny Pea **Bob Beet**

☞ Begin titles of a person, such as *Ms.*, *Mr.*, and *Dr.*, with a capital letter.

Miss Cress **Dr. Pickle**

☞ Capitalize initials that take the place of names.

Hazel R. Nut **Susan B. Daisy**

☞ Always capitalize the word *I*.

Penny Pea and I got married.

Practice

✎ Read each sentence. Circle the letters that should be capital letters.

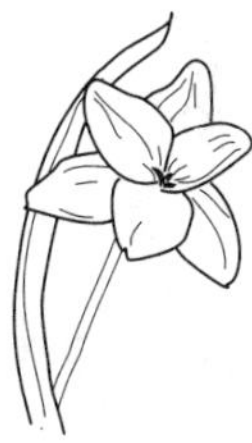

1. "Where's the car?" asked samantha star.

2. "Who will drive?" said ed endive.

3. "I have a rig!" yelled mr. Fig.

4. "Where will we go?" asked ms. Avocado.

5. "To the church," said dr. Birch.

6. "The bride is late," said j. r. Date.

7. "The music is nice," whispered t. c. Rice.

8. "Here they come," said Pam g. Plum.

9. "They'll say i will," said Daffodil.

10. "They'll say i do," said Ben Bamboo.

Name ______________________ Date ______________

Naturally Named

☞ Begin the name of a town, city, state, and country with a capital letter.

Lima, Ohio	**Appleton, Wisconsin**
United States	**France**

☞ Begin the name of a street and its abbreviation with a capital letter.

Pinetree street—St.	**Rose Road—Rd.**
Clover Avenue—Ave.	**Daisy Boulevard—Blvd.**

Practice

✎ Read each sentence. Circle the letters that should be capital letters.

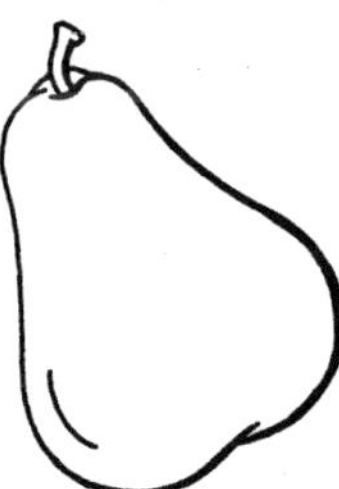

1. Mrs. Begonia travels to bologna, italy.
2. Joseph Berry drives to cherry hill, new jersey.
3. Does Ms. Lime live in lyme, connecticut?
4. Sarah Sloe will move to boise, idaho.
5. Her friend, Mr. Pear, lives in dover, delaware.
6. Mr. Oak lives on forest avenue.
7. Dr. Lilac built a house on larkspur lane.
8. Mr. Acorn's shop is found on squash blvd.
9. Ms. Dill lives on walnut hill.
10. Mr. Beet has a house on turnip street.
11. green road is Miss Cress's address.
12. Mr. Cherry lives on strawberry lane.

Name ______________________________ Date ______________

Days, Months, and Holidays

☞ Begin the name of a day of the week or its abbreviation with a capital letter.

Monday—Mon.	**Friday—Fri.**

☞ Begin the name of the month or its abbreviation with a capital letter.

February—Feb.	**August—Aug.**

☞ Begin each important word in the name of a holiday with a capital letter.

Fourth of July	**Labor Day**

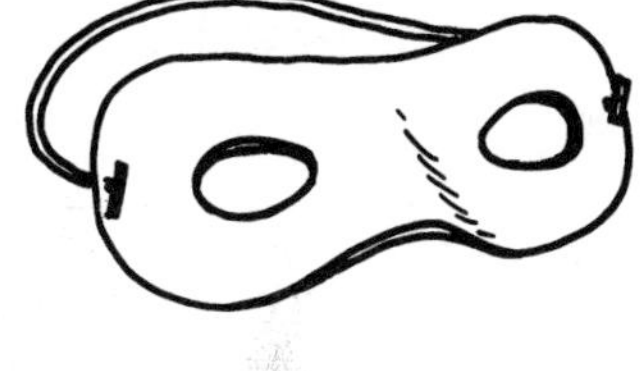

Practice

✎ Read each sentence. Circle the letters that should be capital letters.

1. Amelia went to the World's Fair on monday, october 11.
2. Amelia tried the roller coaster on wednesday.
3. friday they toured the fair's "White City."
4. The World's Fair opened in october.
5. Many people went to the fair in november.
6. Amelia spent columbus day at the fair.
7. On halloween Amelia wore a mask she bought at the fair.
8. Amelia still talked about the fair on thanksgiving day.

Name ______________________________ Date ______________

Correct Capitals

☞ Use a capital letter to begin the first word in a sentence.

The salt mist touched Manny and Tony.

☞ Use a capital letter to begin the first, last, and all important words in the title of a book, story, song, or poem.

Marvin and the Mole (book)

"The Grasshopper" (poem)

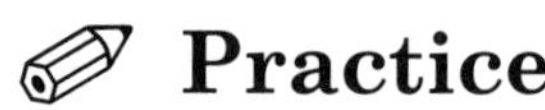

Practice

A. Write each sentence correctly. Add capital letters where they are needed.

1. tony and Manny are best friends.

____

2. they have been friends for a long time.

____

3. they play basketball.

____

4. sometimes they go fishing.

____

B. Write each sentence correctly. Add capital letters to the important words in each title.

5. Is there a snake in the poem "that's me"?

____

6. You will enjoy reading the book beautiful bugs and other creatures.

____

Name ______________________________ Date ______________

Using Periods

☞ Use a period (.) at the end of a statement or a command.

Manny and Tony like the beach.
Don't pinch me anymore.

☞ Use a period after an abbreviation.

Mr. Smith swims in the summer.
He visits his friend Dr. Quick.

☞ Use a period after a numeral in the main topic of an outline.

<u>Wind Power</u>

I. Using wind power on the sea
II. Using wind power on land

Practice

✎ Read each item. Add periods where they are needed.

1. Manny and Tony go to the beach every day
2. They take a picnic lunch
3. Do not step on the crabs
4. Dr Quick looked at Mr Smith's toe.
5. Mrs Smith found a bandage.
6. Dr Quick helped Mr Smith.
7. <u>Beach Activities</u>

   I Play in the waves

   II Look for shells

   III Have a picnic

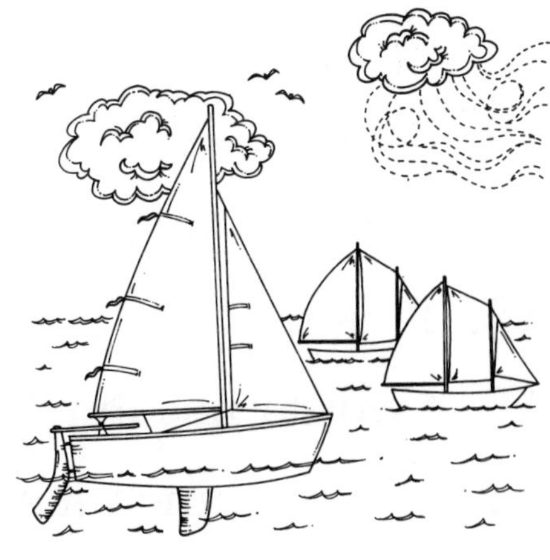

Name ______________________________ Date ______________

Using Question Marks and Exclamation Points

☞ Use a question mark (?) at the end of a question.

What is a mole?

☞ Use an exclamation point (!) at the end of an exclamation.

That is some troll!

Practice

✏ Read each sentence. Add a question mark or an exclamation point at the end of each sentence.

1. What is your favorite place
2. Do you have a beach house
3. Who is your best friend
4. Do you think your friend would pinch you
5. Would you pinch a friend
6. Did you know someone else was at the beach
7. Where did the crab go
8. You pinched me
9. I did not
10. It hurt
11. What happened
12. This is serious
13. I would not pinch you
14. You did pinch me

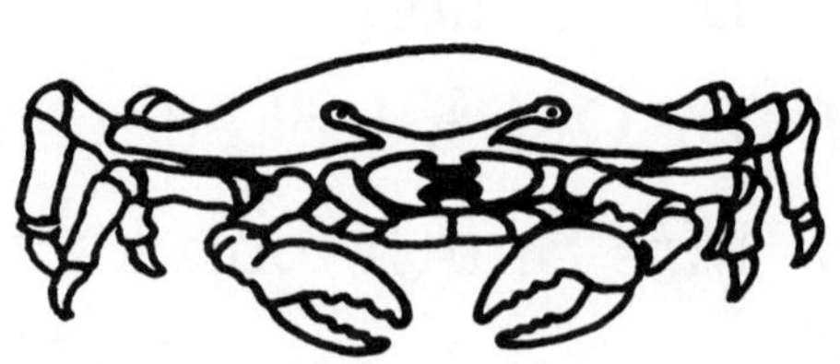

Name ______________________ Date ____________

Using Commas

☞ Use a comma (,) between a city and a state or a city and a country.

Topeka, Kansas	**Osaka, Japan**

☞ Use a comma between the day and the year.

April 1, 1999	**September 17, 2000**

☞ Use a comma after the greeting in a friendly letter and after the closing of any letter.

Dear Mr. Wong,	**Your friend,**

Practice

✎ Read this friendly letter. Add commas where they are needed.

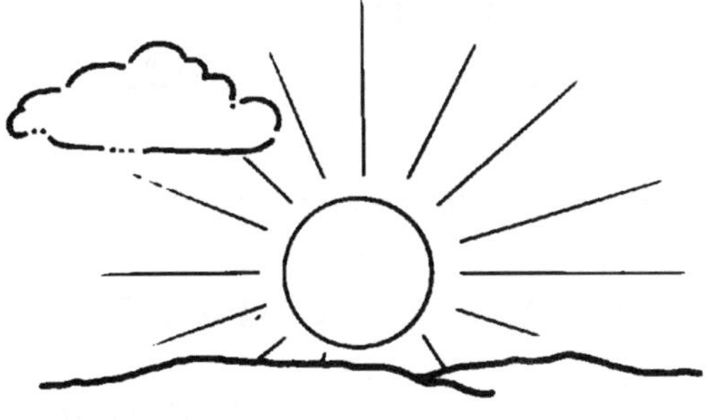

New Delhi India
July 27 1999

Dear Chandra

Today I watched the sun rise from beside the river in our city. As I watched the sun, a beautiful paper boat floated toward the shore. I caught the boat and read your name and address. The shiuli flowers were still fresh. They reminded me of the beauty of the morning. Thank you for sending your boat. It helped me to appreciate the new day and reminded me of forgotten dreams.

May your boats find many new friends for you.

Sincerely
Sadar Rangairi

Name ______________________________ Date ______________

First, Add a Comma

☞ Use a comma (,) after introductory words such as *first* and *next*.

First, we woke up hungry.

Then, I said I was hungry.

☞ Use a comma before the word *and* when two complete sentences are joined together.

We left, and we began hunting for food.

Practice

✎ Read each sentence. Add commas where they are needed.

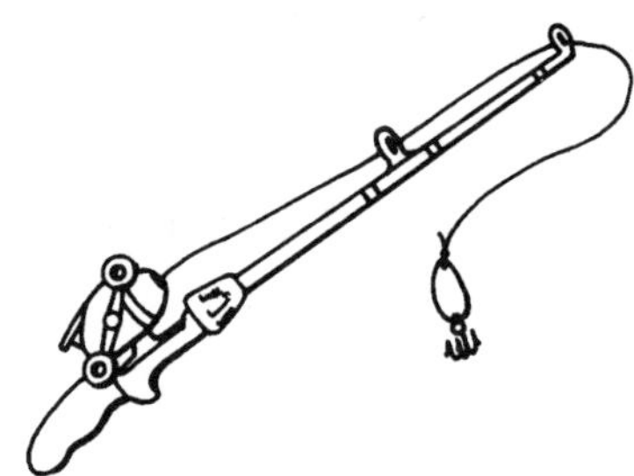

1. First we looked for food by the river.
2. Next we looked in every cave.
3. Then we returned home.
4. First we said we would like some wild berries.
5. Then we thought of a plan.
6. Finally we told the others our idea.
7. We decided to go fishing and we went to the lake.
8. We brought our fishing poles and we brought some bait.
9. We dug a pit and we started a fire.
10. We got the fish ready and we cooked them for dinner.

Name ______________________ Date ______________

Using Colons and Apostrophes

☞ Use a colon (:) between the hour and the minute in the time of day.

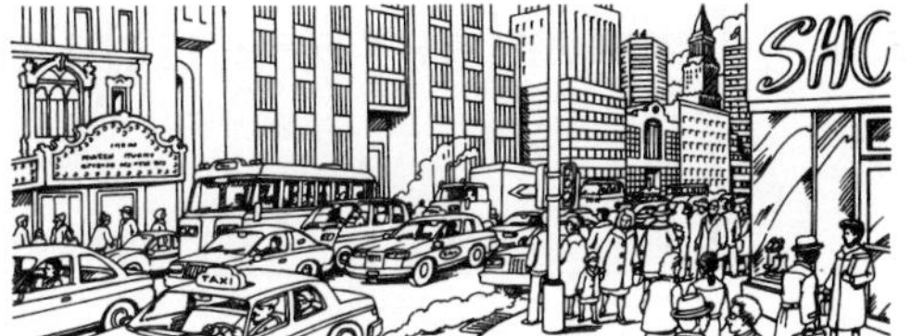

1:15 P.M.	**6:30 A.M.**

☞ Use an apostrophe (') to show that one or more letters have been left out in a contraction.

is not—isn't	**have not—haven't**

☞ Add an apostrophe and an *s* to singular nouns to show possession.

Amelia's project	**Jimmy's secret**

☞ Add an apostrophe to plural nouns that end in *s* to show possession.

girls' laughter	**parents' plan**

Practice

✎ Complete each sentence correctly. Add colons and apostrophes where they are needed.

1. Meghan and her family took the 8 30 P.M. train.
2. At 7 15 the next morning, they ate breakfast.
3. The train pulled into Union Station at 8 45 A.M.
4. Meghan didnt want to waste time.
5. She wasnt interested in looking at the city from their windows.
6. Meghans cousins met them at the hotel.
7. Her cousins rooms overlooked the lake.
8. Meghans father took them to the fair.

Name ______________________________ Date ______________

Using Underlines And Quotation Marks

☞ Underline the title of a book.

The Magic Windmill (book)

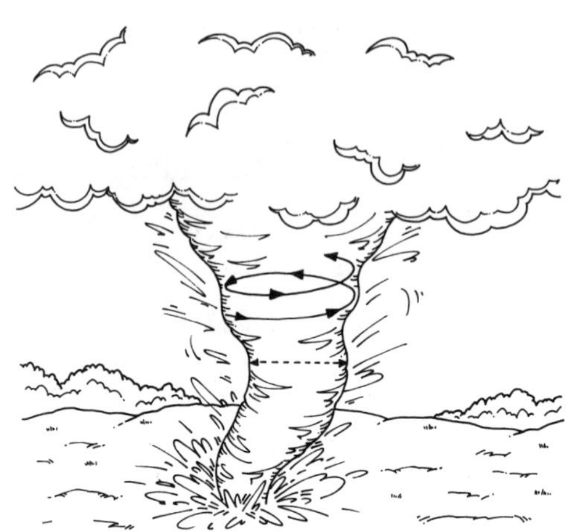

☞ Use quotation marks (" ") before and after the title of a story or a poem.

"Wind in the Orchard" (story)

"Capture the Wind" (poem)

Practice

✏ Read each sentence. Add quotation marks and underlines where they are needed.

1. Find out more about wind power in the book Catch the Wind.
2. Wind power and other kinds of energy are explained in the book Energy All Around.
3. The book Silent Friend, Silent Foe tells about the power of the wind.
4. I need to return the book Storm Track to the library.
5. Who Has Seen the Wind? is a lovely poem.
6. Ten-Dollar Wind is a story about a lost ten-dollar bill.
7. The story Something in the Wind is a mystery.
8. I can hear bells ringing when I read the poem Wind Chimes.

Name ______________________________ Date ______________

Unit Five Assessment: Kinds of Writing

✎ Look at the picture. Choose one of the kinds of writing in the box. Circle your choice. Write about the picture using the kind of writing you chose. Use the back of this paper or another piece of paper for your writing.

Note: Be sure to follow the rules of good writing.

- ☞ If you are writing a story, write a beginning, a middle, and an ending.
- ☞ Give your characters problems to solve.
- ☞ Write clear paragraphs with topic sentences and detail sentences.
- ☞ Give your writing a title.

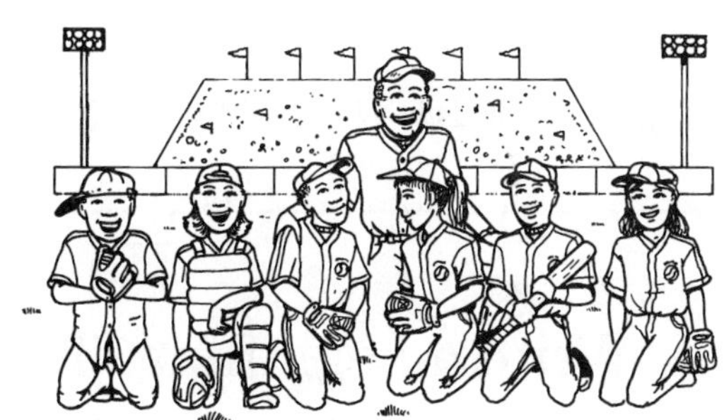

Kinds of Writing

story (beginning, middle, ending; solve a problem)

poem (paint a picture with words; use *rhyme* and *rhythm*)

news story (tell about an event; tell *who, what, when, where, why*)

magazine article (nonfiction; give information about a topic)

friendly letter (use *heading, greeting, body, closing, signature*)

invitation (tell *who, what, when, where,* and *special information*)

journal (write date; list important events)

Name ______________________ Date ____________

What's the Story?

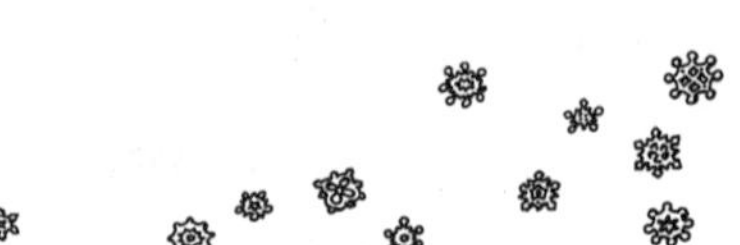

☞ In a **story** a writer tells about one main idea. Every story has a **beginning**, a **middle**, and an **ending**.

A New Home

One winter day Pablo Possum decided that his log was too cold. He waited for his friend Rose Mary to open the door of her house. Then he raced inside. Pablo ran from room to room, looking for a warm hiding place. He found the perfect spot in a basket full of clothes. Pablo did not worry about cold weather again.

How to Write a Story

1. Write a beginning. Tell who the story is about and where the story takes place.
2. Write the middle. Tell what the characters do. Give them problems to solve.
3. Write the ending. Tell how the characters solve their problems.
4. Give your story a title.

Practice

✎ Write another ending for the example story above.

____

____

____

____

____

Name ______________________________ Date ______________

Word Art

☞ In a **poem** a writer paints a picture with words. Poems often describe something in an unusual or interesting way. Many poems also have **rhyming words**. The words in a poem often have a definite **rhythm,** or **beat.**

"Sea Gifts"

The wave tossed gifts upon the shore
Treasures from the deep—
Shells, crabs, driftwood, and more
For me to find and keep.

How to Write a Poem

1. Choose a topic for your poem.
2. Use colorful words to paint a picture.
3. Use rhyme and rhythm to express feelings.
4. Give your poem a title.

Practice

✎ Finish the poem. Think of colorful words and words that rhyme. Write another verse for the poem. Then make up a title for it.

The frog wants a drink.
He hops into the sink.
The ________________ water comes down.
Will the ________________ frog ________________?

____

____

____

____

Name ______________________________ Date ______________

News Flash!

☞ In a **news story** a writer tells about an event. A news story answers the questions *who, what, when, where,* and sometimes *why.*

☞ The **headline** is the title of a news story.

Derby Opens New Shoe Factory

Angus Derby has announced the grand opening of a new Derby Shoe Factory in Edinburgh, Scotland. The grand opening celebration will be on November 10 at 7:30 P.M. The new factory is opening because there has been such a demand for shocking shoes. At the grand opening, another secret line of shoes will be introduced.

How to Write a News Story

1. Write a sentence that introduces the story.
2. Give details that tell *who, what, when,* and *where.*
3. Write a short headline. Use a strong verb. Begin each important word in the headline with a capital letter.

Practice

✎ On another sheet of paper or the back of this one, write a news story about the grand opening. Add detail sentences that tell *who, what, when,* and *where* about this topic sentence.

A new line of shoes called "Derby Dippers" is now made at the new Derby Shoe Factory.

Name ______________________ Date ______________

Camp Commotion

☞ In a **magazine article** a writer gives information about a topic. Many magazine articles are **nonfiction**. This means the information in the article is true.

Crawly Company

People who plan to camp should be prepared for some crawly company. Spiders surprise campers by appearing in unusual places. Spiders can be found on early morning canoe trips. They might jump out of boots, drop from trees, or crawl out from under rocks. Campers should expect to find spiders in tents, in woodpiles, and even in backpacks.

How to Write a Magazine Article

1. Choose a topic and find out about it.
2. Write a topic sentence that tells about the main idea.
3. Put your information in order. Be sure the detail sentences tell about the main idea.
4. Write an interesting title for your article.

Practice

✎ Finish this chart. Write where spiders are found. Use the example magazine article to help you.

Spiders Are Everywhere		

Name ______________________ Date ______________

Between Friends

☞ In a **friendly letter** a writer writes to someone he or she knows. A friendly letter has five parts.

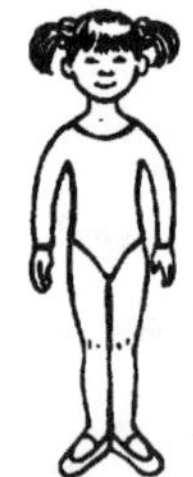

8 Elm Drive ← **heading**
Ames, Iowa 50010
May 6, 1999

Dear Wendy, ← **greeting**

Today I started ballet lessons. The tutu made me feel like a ballerina even though I couldn't dance. I already feel more graceful. How are your painting lessons? ← **body**

Your friend, ← **closing**

Geraldine ← **signature**

How to Write a Friendly Letter

1. Write the heading and greeting correctly.
2. Write a friendly message in the body.
3. Write the closing correctly.
4. Sign the letter with your name.

Practice

✎ Think of two more sentences that you could add to the example friendly letter. Then write the sentences.

____

____

____

Name ______________________________ Date ______________

You're Invited!

☞ In an **invitation** a writer asks the reader to come somewhere.

heading 63 Topeka Road
Ace, Kansas 66002
July 10, 1999

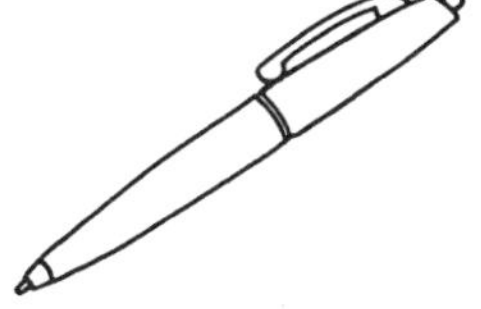

greeting Dear Lucy,

body Please help me build a new ride on Thursday, July 12. We will begin at 9:30 A.M. near the barn. We will work until lunch at 12:30 P.M.

closing Your cousin,

signature Amelia

How to Write an Invitation

1. Tell *who* is invited.
2. Tell *what* the invitation is for.
3. Tell *when* to come and *where* the event is.
4. Tell any special information your guest needs.

Practice

✏ Read the example invitation. Think of two more sentences you could add to it. Then write the sentences.

____

____

____

Name ______________________________ Date ______________

Thank-You!

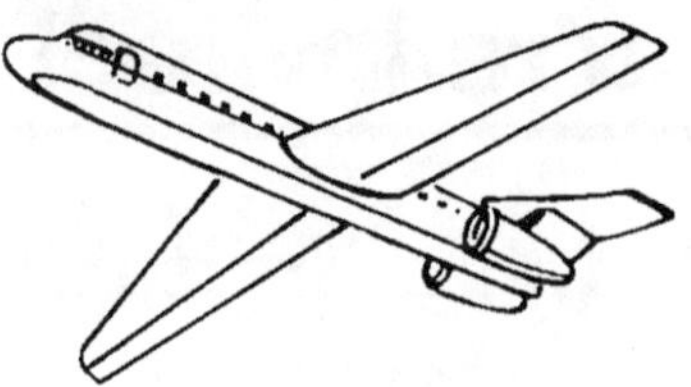

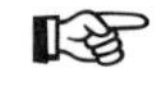 In a **thank-you note** a writer thanks someone for a gift or a special favor.

12 Peachtree Lane Jacksonville, Florida 30021 June 12, 1999	**heading**
Dear Father,	**greeting**
Thank you for sending me the plane ticket. I can't wait to see you. I hope I will always be as thoughtful as you are.	**body**
Your daughter,	**closing**
Belinda	**signature**

How to Write a Thank-You Note

1. Tell what you are thanking the person for.
2. If you have been a guest at someone's house, tell why you enjoyed yourself.
3. If you received a gift, say how you are using it.

Practice

List at least three reasons why you might write a thank-you note.

____

____

____

____

Name ______________________________ Date ______________

Address an Envelope

☞ An **envelope** is used to send a letter or a note.

☞ The receiver's **address** goes toward the center. The **return address** is in the upper left corner.

☞ **Postal abbreviations** are used for state names.

☞ The **ZIP Code** goes after the state abbreviation.

return address → Geraldine Roberts
8 Maple Drive
Camp Hill, PA 17011

stamp

receiver's name and address → Wendy Garrison
220 Arlington Ave
Bolivar, NY 14715

Postal Abbreviations

State	Abbr.	State	Abbr.	State	Abbr.
Alabama	AL	Kentucky	KY	North Dakota	ND
Alaska	AK	Louisiana	LA	Ohio	OH
Arizona	AZ	Maine	ME	Oklahoma	OK
Arkansas	AR	Maryland	MD	Oregon	OR
California	CA	Massachusetts	MA	Pennsylvania	PA
Colorado	CO	Michigan	MI	Rhode Island	RI
Connecticut	CT	Minnesota	MN	South Carolina	SC
Delaware	DE	Mississippi	MS	South Dakota	SD
District of Columbia	DC	Missouri	MO	Tennessee	TN
Florida	FL	Montana	MT	Texas	TX
Georgia	GA	Nebraska	NE	Utah	UT
Hawaii	HI	Nevada	NV	Vermont	VT
Idaho	ID	New Hampshire	NH	Virginia	VA
Illinois	IL	New Jersey	NJ	Washington	WA
Indiana	IN	New Mexico	NM	West Virginia	WV
Iowa	IA	New York	NY	Wisconsin	WI
Kansas	KS	North Carolina	NC	Wyoming	WY

Practice

✏ Choose a partner. Draw an envelope on another piece of paper. Address it from yourself to your partner.

Name ____________________ Date ____________

Keep a Journal

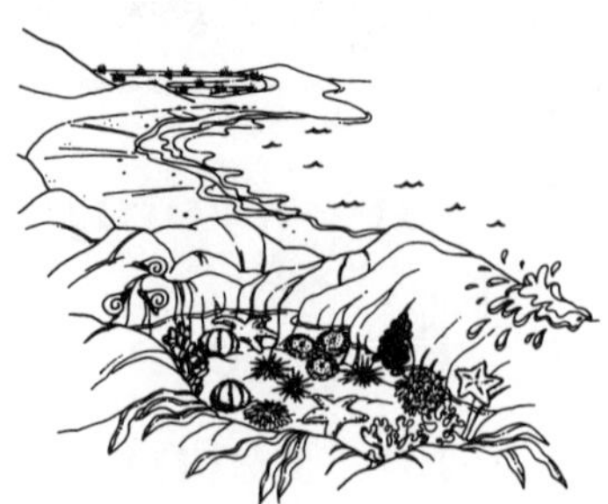

 In a **journal** a writer keeps a record of daily events. The daily record is called an **entry**. Writers often use their journals for ideas.

April 5, 1999

Today I went to the beach with my family. I saw our friends Joe and Danielle near a tide pool. They looked angry. I wonder what happened. I hope Joe and Danielle are still friends. Friends are good to have.

How to Write a Journal Entry

1. Write a date.
2. Write one or two important things that happened that day.
3. Explain why the events are important to you.

Practice

Write a journal entry that tells about something you saw and how you felt yesterday.

____

____

____

____

____

____

Name ______________________ Date ______________

How Was Your Book?

☞ In a **book report** a writer tells about the important events in a book. The writer also gives his or her opinion of the book.

Title Rufus M.

Author Eleanor Estes

About the Book Rufus Moffat wants to take a book out of the library. He is four years old, so this is not an easy thing for him to do. Rufus cannot fill out a library card application. Will Rufus ever be able to take out a book?

Opinion I liked this book. I liked the way Rufus kept trying.

How to Write a Book Report

1. Write the title of the book. Underline it.
2. Give the author's name.
3. Tell about the book. Tell the main idea and interesting details. Do not tell the ending.
4. Give your opinion of the book.

Practice

✎ Read the example book report. Write a report about a book you have read. Use the back of this paper or another sheet of paper.

Name ______________________________ Date ______________

Unit Six Assessment: Paragraphs

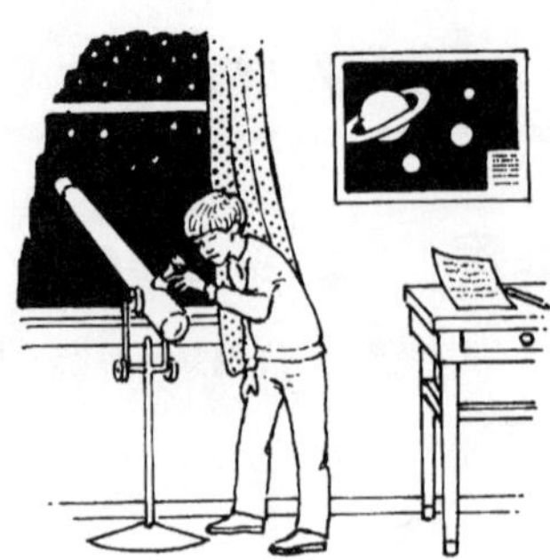

✏ Look at the picture. Choose one of the kinds of paragraphs in the box. Circle your choice. Write a paragraph about the picture using the kind of paragraph writing you chose.

Note: Be sure to follow the rules for a good paragraph.

☞ Indent your first line.

☞ Write a topic sentence that tells the main idea.

☞ Write detail sentences that tell more about the main idea.

Kinds of Paragraphs

how-to paragraph (uses *first, next, then,* and *last*)
comparing paragraph (how things are alike)
contrasting paragraph (how things are different)
information paragraph (tells why things happen)
defining paragraph (tells what something means)
describing paragraph (uses describing words)
persuading paragraph (tells how you feel about something)

____

____

____

____

____

____

____

Name ______________________ Date ______________

What's a Paragraph?

☞ A **paragraph** is a group of sentences that tells about one main idea. The first line of a paragraph is **indented**. This means the first word is moved in a little from the left margin.

☞ The **topic sentence** tells the main idea of the paragraph.

☞ The other sentences in a paragraph are the **detail sentences**. Detail sentences tell about the main idea.

Hunter spiders hunt for their food. Some hunters use their teeth to catch food. Other hunters run to trap food. Some jump on insects to catch them.

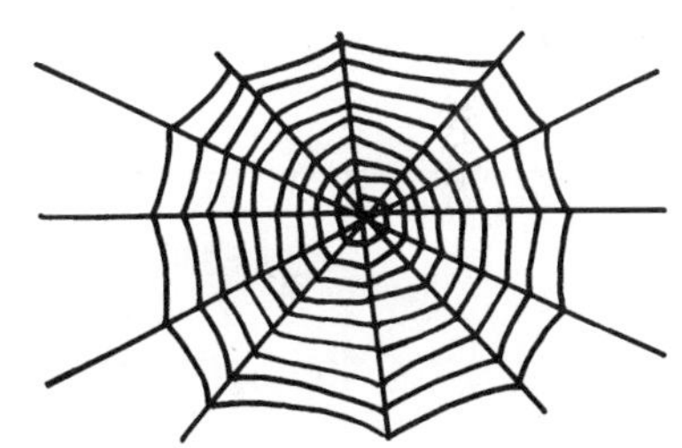

How to Write a Paragraph

1. Write a topic sentence that clearly tells the main idea of your paragraph.
2. Indent the first line.
3. Write detail sentences that tell about the main idea.

Practice

✎ Read the example paragraph. List three details that tell about the main idea.

____

____

____

Name ______________________ Date ____________

How Do You Do It?

☞ In a **how-to paragraph** a writer gives directions that tell how to do something in order.

Here is how to catch flies. Get a rubber band and a jar with holes in the lid. First, sneak up on the fly slowly. Next, put the rubber band over the index finger of one hand. With your other hand, pull back the rubber band. Then aim and let go. Finally, if you stun a fly, put it in the jar.

How to Write a How-To Paragraph

1. Write a topic sentence that tells what you are going to explain.
2. Add a detail sentence that tells what materials are needed.
3. Write detail sentences that tell the steps in the directions.
4. Use time-order words such as *first, next, then,* and *last* to show correct order.

Practice

✎ Read the example paragraph. List each step that tells how to catch a fly.

1. ______________________
2. ______________________
3. ______________________
4. ______________________
5. ______________________

Name ______________________________ Date ______________

How Are They Alike?

☞ In a **comparing paragraph** a writer can show how two people, places, or things are alike.

Geese and California grey whales are alike because they migrate and because they travel in large groups. First, both geese and whales migrate thousands of miles. Second, both geese and whales travel in large groups to reach warmer weather. Geese migrate in groups called flocks. Whales travel in groups called pods.

How to Write a Paragraph That Tells How Things Are Alike

1. Write a topic sentence that names the subjects and tells how they are alike.
2. Give clear examples in the detail sentences.
3. Write about each subject in the same order in which you named it in the topic sentence.

Practice

✏ Read the example paragraph. List details that tell how geese and whales are alike.

____

____

____

____

____

____

Name ______________________________ Date ______________

How Are They Different?

☞ In a **contrasting paragraph** a writer can show how two people, places, or things are different.

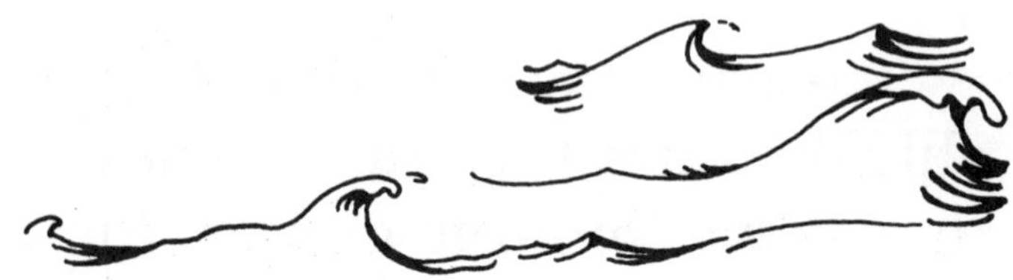

Arctic terns and bobolinks are birds that have different habits during migration. Arctic terns fly mainly over water. Bobolinks fly mostly over land. Along the way, Arctic terns dive into the water to feed on fish. Bobolinks hunt on land for insects and grain.

How to Write a Paragraph That Tells How Things Are Different

1. Write a topic sentence that names the subjects and tells how they are different.
2. Give examples in the detail sentences that clearly tell how the subjects are different.
3. Write about each difference in the same order you used in the topic sentence.

Practice

✎ Read the example paragraph. List ways in which the Arctic tern and the bobolink are different.

____

____

____

____

____

Name ______________________________ Date ______________

Why Did It Happen?

☞ In an **information paragraph** a writer explains why something happened.

Many Indians chose to live near rivers. The rivers provided drinking water. The Indians hunted for food in the rivers. Also, the rich soil next to a river was perfect for planting crops.

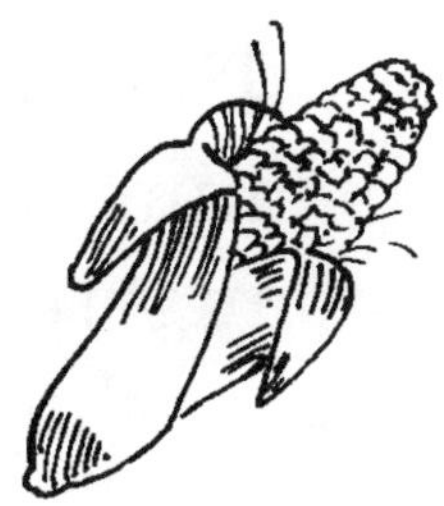

How to Write an Information Paragraph

1. Write a topic sentence that tells what happened.
2. Write detail sentences that explain why this happened.

Practice

✏ Finish this drawing. Write why Indians decided to live by rivers. Use the example information paragraph.

What Happened ______________________________

Why It Happened

Name ______________________ Date ______________

Tell All About It

☞ In a **definition paragraph** a writer tells the meaning of an idea or a word.

The word *rescue* has a very special meaning for some animals. To rescue endangered animals means more than saving their lives. Animal rescuers must also protect the animals' homes and food supplies. The rescuers make sure that forests are protected. They check that water supplies are fresh.

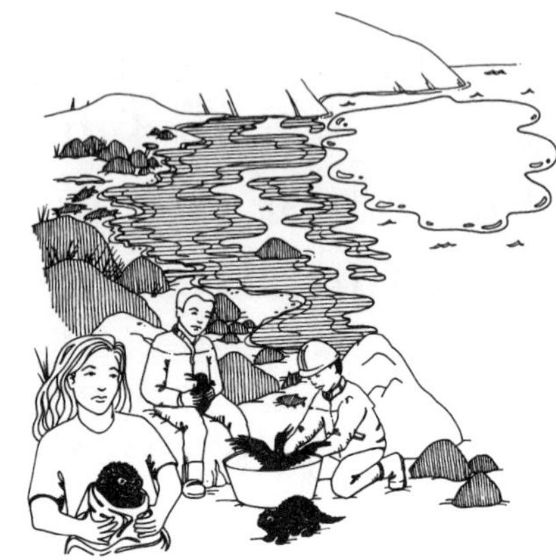

How to Write a Definition Paragraph

1. Choose a word or idea to explain.
2. Tell what you will explain in the topic sentence.
3. Use clear examples to tell the meaning of the topic.
4. Use exact words to make your examples clear to the reader.

Practice

✎ Read the example paragraph. Write examples that tell what *rescue* means.

____

____

____

____

____

____

Name ______________________ Date ______________

What Is It Like?

☞ In a **descriptive paragraph** a writer describes a person, place, thing, or event. It should let the reader *see, feel, hear,* and sometimes *taste* or *smell* what is being described.

An interesting animal is the desert tortoise. Desert tortoises have a special way to keep cool. Their large, heavy shells protect them from the hot sun. The shells also store extra water.

How to Write a Descriptive Paragraph

1. Write a topic sentence that clearly tells what the paragraph is about.
2. Add detail sentences. Use colorful words to give information about your topic.
3. Make an exact picture for the reader with the words you choose.

Practice

✎ Read the example paragraph. List descriptive words that give a clearer picture.

____

____

____

____

____

____

____

Name ______________________ Date ______________

What Is Your Opinion?

☞ In some paragraphs a writer tells his or her feelings, or **opinions**, about a topic.

I feel the miller in "Rumpelstiltskin" was a thoughtless father. He lied about his daughter to the king. The miller did not think about what the king would do when he found out. The miller should have told the king true, good things about his daughter.

How to Write a Paragraph That Tells About Feelings

1. Write a topic sentence that tells your feelings.
2. In the detail sentences give reasons that show why you feel as you do.
3. Remember your reader as you write.

Practice

✎ Finish this chart. Tell what the writer's feelings were and the reasons for those feelings. Use the example paragraph.

Feeling	
Reason	**Reason**

Name ______________________________ Date ________________

Convince Me!

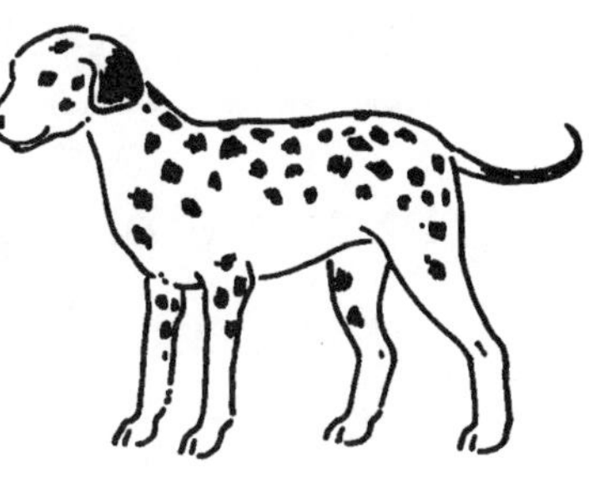

☞ In some paragraphs a writer tries to **convince** the reader to agree with his or her feelings about a topic. This is called *persuading*.

I think the word <u>dog</u> should be replaced with <u>woofer</u>. Dog has nothing to do with the way the animal looks, acts, or sounds. I think people should use the name <u>woofer</u> because <u>woof</u> is the sound dogs make! The next time you see a dog, be sure to call it a woofer.

How to Write a Paragraph That Convinces

1. Write a topic sentence that tells your feelings.
2. Give reasons to support your feelings in the detail sentences. Save your strongest reason for last.
3. At the end of your paragraph, tell your feelings again. Then ask your reader to feel the same way.

Practice

✏ Read the example paragraph. List the writer's feeling and three reasons that support it.

____

____

____

____

____

____

Name ______________________________ Date ______________

What About You?

☞ In some paragraphs a writer tells about his or her life.

When I was four, I wanted to fill out an application for a library card. First, I wrote my name. The librarian could not read it. So she taught me how to print my name. Then, I proudly filled out the application.

How to Write a Paragraph That Tells About Yourself
1. Tell about yourself. Use the pronouns *I, me,* and *my* to tell about yourself.
2. Write about events in order. Use time-order words.

Practice

✎ Think about something that has happened to you. Tell about what happened to you in a paragraph. Write at least three sentences.

____

____

____

____

____

____

____

____

Name ______________________________ Date ______________

Unit Seven Assessment: Resource Materials and Research

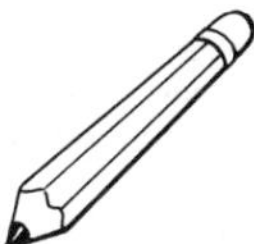

Use the example book pages to answer the questions.

title page	table of contents	index
ART PROJECTS AT THE BEACH by Sandy Shore Crafts Books, Inc.	**Contents** Getting Started 8 Shell Art 10 Sand Art 32 Sea-Plant and Rock Crafts 50	Beaches, 8–10, 26, 29 Plants, 50–54, 60–62 Rocks, 50–54, 59–62 Sand, 8–12, 32–49 Shells, 8, 10–30

1. What is the title of the book? ______________________
2. On what page is Sand Art? ______________________
3. On what pages would you find facts about shells? __________

Tell if each book is *fiction* or *nonfiction*.

4. a book of maps ______________________
5. a story about a talking animal ______________________

Use the example dictionary page to answer these questions.

> **cherry** — **chip**
>
> **cher·ry** [cher'ē] *n., pl.* **cher·ries** **1** A small, round, eatable fruit, red, yellow, or nearly black in color, and having a single pit. **2** The tree bearing this fruit. **3** The wood of this tree. **4** A bright red color.
>
> **child** [chīld] *n., pl.* **chil·dren** [chil'dren] **1** A baby. **2** A young boy or girl. **3** A son or daughter. **4** A person from a certain family.

6. What are the guide words on this page? ______________
7. Would the word *chin* be on this page? ______________

Use an encyclopedia to find information on your favorite animal. Take notes, then use the information you find to write a paragraph about the animal. Use the back of this paper or another piece of paper for your work.

Name ______________________________ Date ______________

What's in a Book?

☞ The **title page** tells the name of a book. It gives the name of the author. It also tells the name of the company that published the book.

☞ The **table of contents** comes after the title page. It lists the titles of the chapters or units in the book. It also lists the page on which each new part begins. Everything in the book is listed in the order in which it appears.

☞ An **index** is a list of all the topics in a book. It is in alphabetical order. It lists the page or pages on which each topic appears.

Practice

✎ Use the example book pages to answer these questions.

ART PROJECTS
AT THE BEACH
by
Sandy Shore

Crafts Books, Inc.

title page

Contents

Getting Started	8
Shell Art	10
Sand Art	32
Sea-Plant and Rock Crafts	50

table of contents

Beaches, 8–10, 26, 29
Plants, 50–54, 60–62
Rocks, 50–54, 59–62
Sand, 8–12, 32–49
Shells, 8, 10–30

index

1. What is the title of the book? ______________________
2. Who wrote the book? ______________________
3. What company published this book? ______________________
4. What is the first chapter in the book? ______________________
5. On what pages would you find facts about beaches?

____

Name ______________________________ Date ______________

True or Make-Believe?

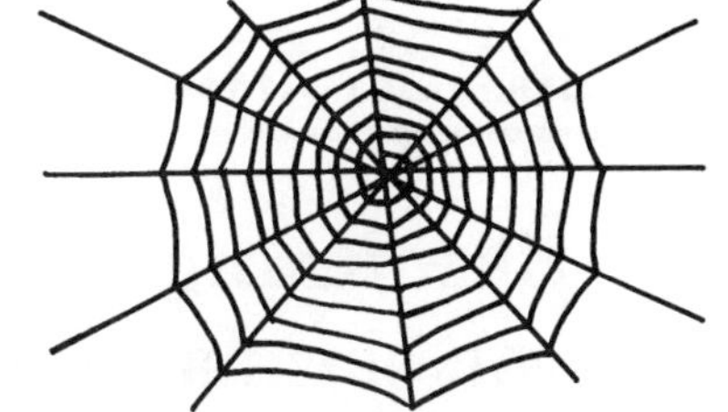

☞ **Fiction** books tell stories. They tell about make-believe people and things.

***Charlotte's Web*—a book about a talking spider**

☞ **Nonfiction** books tell facts about real people, things, or events. A nonfiction book that tells about the life of a real person is called a **biography**.

***Spider Silk*—facts about how spiders spin webs**

☞ A **card catalog** is a set of cards that lists every book in the library. The cards in the card catalog are in alphabetical order. You can use the card catalog to find books. Most card catalogs are now on computers.

Practice

A. Tell if each book below is *fiction* or *nonfiction*.

1. a book of maps ______________________

2. a true book about a famous scientist's life

____

3. a book of facts about insects of the world

____

4. a story about Lydia, a hamster who talks __________

B. Tell the letter of the alphabet you would use to find these subjects in the card catalogue.

5. spider ______________ **8.** insects ______________

6. pets ______________ **9.** bugs ______________

7. web ______________ **10.** flowers ______________

Name ______________________ Date ______________

A Quick Study

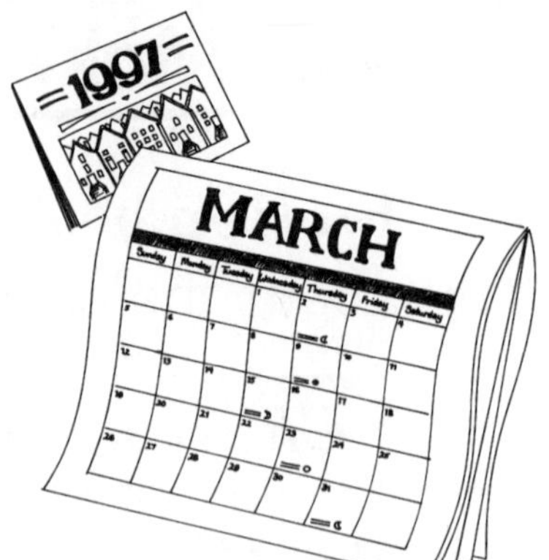

☞ **Skimming** is a quick way to read. When you skim a paragraph, you look for its main idea. The main idea is the most important idea in the paragraph.

☞ **Scanning** is also a quick reading method. When you scan a page, you look it over to find a particular fact.

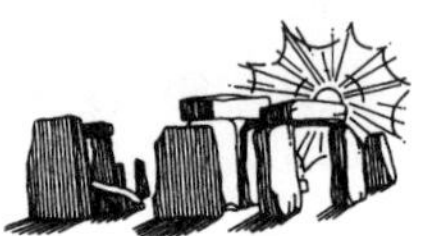

Practice

A. Skim this paragraph. Then circle the sentence below that best states the main idea.

The months of January and March were named after Roman gods long ago. The month of January was named for Janus, the god of beginnings. March was named for Mars, the god of war.

1. Some months are named after Roman gods.
2. The names of the months come from unusual words.
3. The Romans named the months long ago.

B. Scan this paragraph. Then answer the questions.

Other months' names came from Latin words used by Romans. April comes from the Latin word aperio, which means "to open." The last four months of the year come from Latin words for numbers: septem (seven), octo (eight), novem (nine), decem (ten).

4. What does the Latin word aperio mean? ______________
5. What Latin word means the number eight? ______________

Name ______________________________ Date ______________

In the Dictionary

☞ The order of letters from **A** to **Z** is called **alphabetical order**. Words in a dictionary are listed in alphabetical order.

☞ When words begin with the same letters, the next letter of the word is used to put the words in alphabetical order.

cape	**chapel**	**chime**

☞ There are two **guide words** at the top of every dictionary page. The word on the left is the first word on the page. The word on the right is the last word. All the other words on the page are in alphabetical order between the guide words.

☞ Each word in the dictionary is an **entry word.**

Practice

✎ Use the example dictionary page to answer these questions.

cherry **chip**

cher·ry [cher′ē] *n., pl.* **cher·ries** **1** A small, round, eatable fruit, red, yellow, or nearly black in color, and having a single pit. **2** The tree bearing this fruit. **3** The wood of this tree. **4** A bright red color.

child [chīld] *n., pl.* **chil·dren** [chil′dren] **1** A baby. **2** A young boy or girl. **3** A son or daughter. **4** A person from a certain family.

1. What is the last word on this page? ______________
   How do you know? ______________
2. Which of these words would come before cherry in the dictionary:

   carrot, corn, cactus, and clover? ______________

3. Would the word chop be on this page? ______________

Name ______________________ Date ____________

Dictionary Skills

☞ A **syllable** is a word part that has only one vowel sound. Each entry word in the dictionary is divided into syllables.

☞ A **pronunciation** follows each entry word. It shows how to say the word. It also shows the number of syllables in the word.

phlox [floks]	**spinach [spin´ich]**

☞ The **pronunciation key** lists the symbol for each sound. It also gives a familiar word in which the sound is heard. A pronunciation key usually appears on every other page.

a	add	**i**	it	**o͝o**	took	**oi**	oil
ā	ace	**ī**	ice	**o͞o**	pool	**ou**	pout
â	care	**o**	odd	**u**	up	**ng**	ring
ä	palm	**ō**	open	**û**	burn	**th**	thin
e	end	**ô**	order	**yo͞o**	fuse	**th**	this
ē	equal					**zh**	vision

ə = a in *above*, e in *sicken*, i in *possible*, o in *melon*, u in *circus*

Practice

✎ Read each pronunciation. Choose and circle the word that matches the pronunciation. Then tell how many syllables are in each word.

1. klō´vər	clever	cover	clover	______
2. bēt	beet	bet	bait	______
3. pik´əl	pickle	pocket	pluck	______
4. pâr	purr	pear	pour	______
5. (h)wēt	what	wait	wheat	______

Name ______________________________ Date ______________

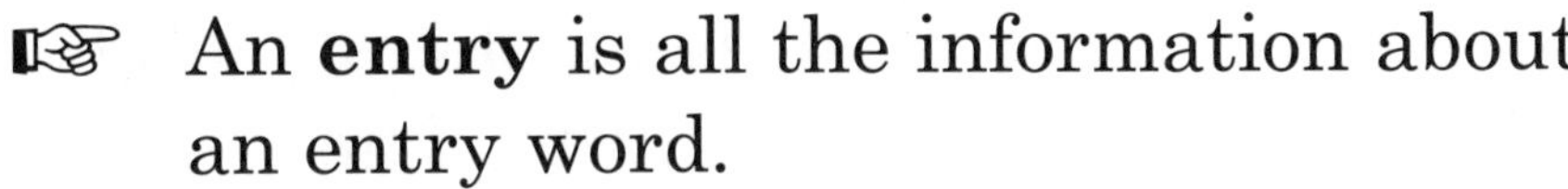

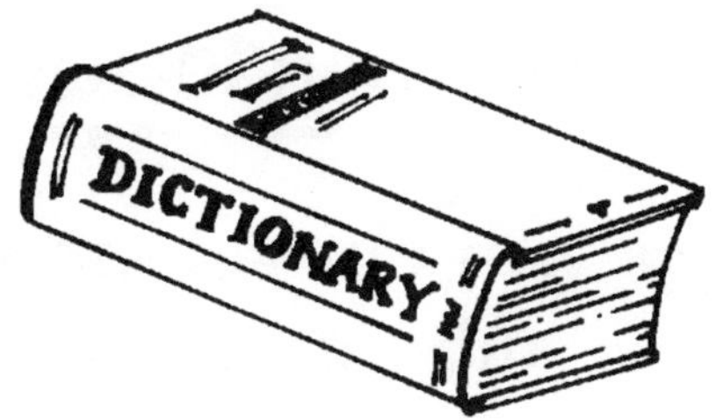

☞ An **entry** is all the information about an entry word.

☞ A **definition** is the meaning of a word. Many words have more than one definition. Each definition is numbered.

☞ A definition is often followed by an **example** that shows how to use the word.

> **spin** [spin] *v.* **1** To draw out and twist (as cotton or flax) into thread. **2** To make fibers into (threads or yarn) by spinning. **3** To make something, as a web or cocoon, from sticky fibers from an insect's body: Wolf spiders do not *spin* webs. **4** To turn or whirl about; rotate: to *spin* a top. **5** To make up a story or tale.

Practice

✎ Use the entry for *spin* to answer the following questions.

1. How many definitions are given for the entry word? ________
2. For which definition is there an example sentence?

   ____

3. How many syllables does the entry word have? ____________
4. What information is given in brackets? [ ] ______________
5. Which definition of *spin* is used in this sentence?

   Rumpelstiltskin could <u>spin</u> straw into gold.

   ____

Name ______________________________ Date ______________

The Encyclopedia

☞ An **encyclopedia** is a set of books that has facts on many subjects. Each book in a set is called a **volume**. The volumes list subjects in alphabetical order.

A	B	C–D	E–F	G–H I	J–K L	M	N–O	P–Q	R–S	T–U V	W–X Y–Z
1	2	3	4	5	6	7	8	9	10	11	12

Practice

A. Use the model encyclopedia to write the number of the volume in which you would find each of these subjects.

1. Mississippi River ________

2. Explorers ______________

3. Rocky Mountains ________

4. Barges __________________

5. Colorado River __________

6. United States ___________

7. Riverboats ______________

8. Farming ________________

B. Write the word or words you would use to look up the following subjects in an encyclopedia.

9. the growth of cities ______________________________

10. the logging business ______________________________

11. mountains in the United States ______________________

12. American ships ______________________________

13. rivers of America ______________________________

14. the uses of water ______________________________

Name ______________________________ Date ______________

Use an Encyclopedia

☞ A set of **encyclopedias** has information on almost any subject that you can imagine. Use an encyclopedia to look up a subject that interests you. Write the name of your subject. Then write some facts about the subject to share with your class.

☞ Remember to write the facts in your own words. Do not copy exactly the words from the encyclopedia.

____

____

____

____

____

____

____

____

____

____

Name ______________________________ Date ______________

Find Your Way

☞ A **map** can show you how to get from one place to another.

☞ A map **key** uses symbols to explain what is shown on the map. A map key may also be called a **legend**.

☞ The **direction symbol**, or **compass rose**, tells you which way is north, south, east, or west on the map.

☞ The **distance scale** shows the distance on the map.

Find Your Way

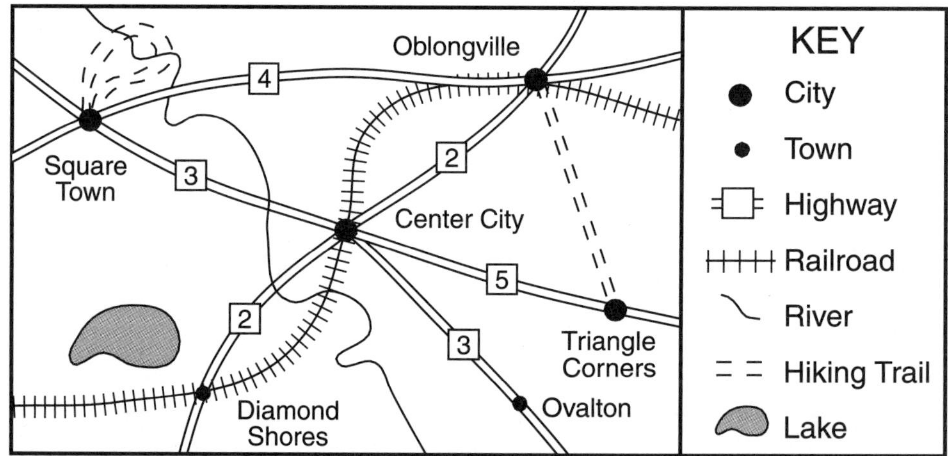

Practice

✎ Use the map to answer the questions.

1. What city do you pass through if you travel from Square Town to Triangle Corners? ______________________
2. Between what two cities is the straight hiking trail?

   ____
3. Near what city is the lake? ______________________

Name ______________________________ Date ______________

Mind Your Map

☞ Use the map below to answer the questions.

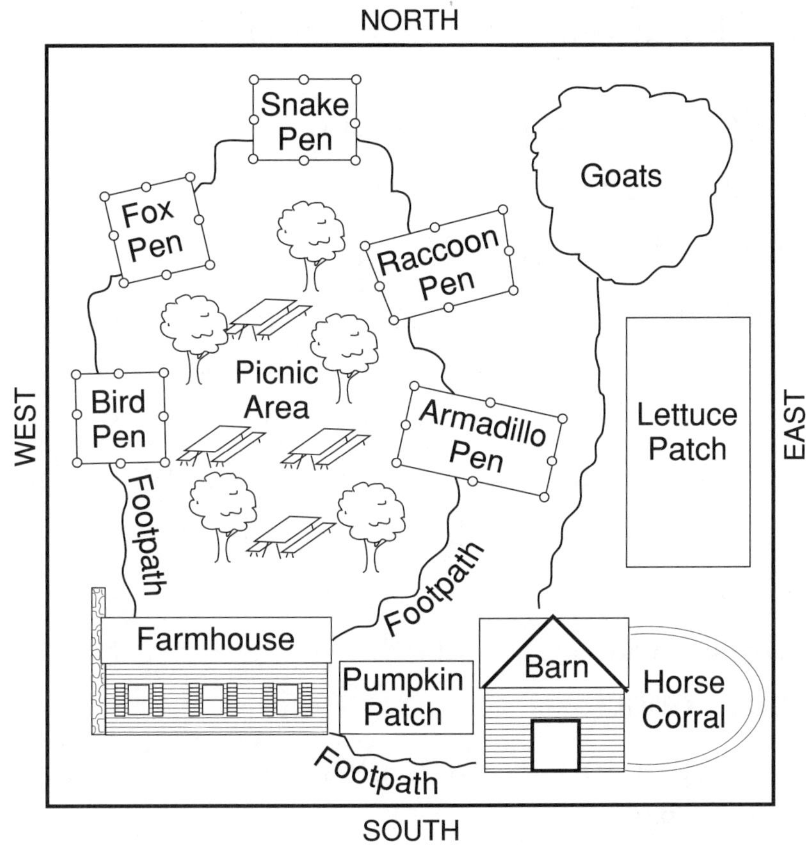

1. If you leave the farmhouse and walk north on the footpath, at which pen do you arrive first? ______________
2. From the Bird Pen, in which direction do you need to walk to get to the Lettuce Patch? ______________
3. In which direction would you walk from the Snake Pen to reach the Pumpkin Patch? ______________
4. What is directly east of the barn? ______________
5. What is directly south of the Raccoon Pen? ______________

Name ______________________________ Date ______________

Take Note!

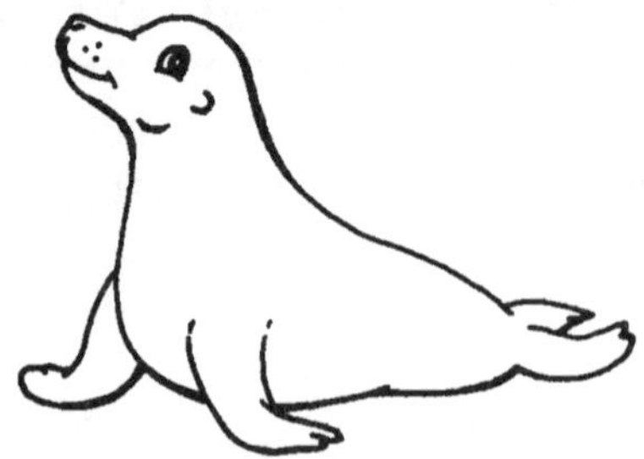

☞ A writer takes good **notes** to remember the facts he or she finds when doing research for a report.

Wild Travelers, by George Laycock, page 67

Where do male fur seals migrate to?

to Gulf of Alaska

travel 400-500 miles from winter home

How to Take Notes

1. Write a question. Then find a book to answer the question.
2. List the title of the book, the author, and the pages where you find facts.
3. Write answers to your question. Write only the facts you need for your report.
4. Write the information in your own words. Write sentences or short groups of words.

Practice

✏ Read this paragraph. Take notes on the facts you would use in a report about female fur seals.

Female fur seals do an amazing thing. Each year in the fall, they migrate 3,000 miles. They leave the Pribilof Islands and swim all the way to southern California.

____

____

____

____

Name ______________________ Date ____________

Make an Outline

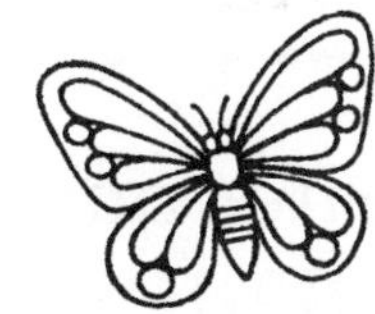

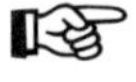 A writer uses an **outline** to put the notes for a research report in order.

Migrating Seals

I. Live in Alaska

II. Travel south in fall

How to Make an Outline

1. Write a title telling the subject of your report.
2. Write the main topics. Use a Roman numeral and a period before each topic.
3. Begin each main topic with a capital letter.

Practice

Write these main topics in correct outline form. Use the title below for your outline.

Migrating Monarch Butterflies

migrate south from Canada and northern United States

spend winter in southern United States and Mexico

return home in spring

____

____

____

____

____

Name ______________________________ Date ______________

Roughing It

☞ A writer quickly puts all of his or her ideas on paper in a **rough draft**.

How to Write a Rough Draft
1. Read your outline and notes. Keep them near you as you write.
2. Follow your outline to write a rough draft. Do not add anything that is not on your outline. Do not leave out anything.
3. Write one paragraph for each Roman numeral in your outline.
4. Write freely. Do not worry about mistakes now. You will make changes later.

Practice

✎ Choose one of the outlines below. Write a topic sentence for each paragraph of a rough draft.

1. <u>Migrating Swallows</u>

I. Fly long distances to get away from cold

II. Migrate by day

III. Travel 10,000 miles

2. <u>Migrating Geese</u>

I. Live in the United States and Canada

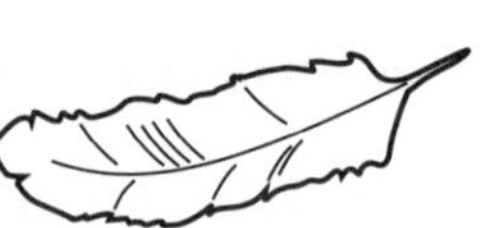

II. Fly in groups

III. Fly as far south as Mexico

____

____

____

____

Name ______________________ Date ______________

Research Report

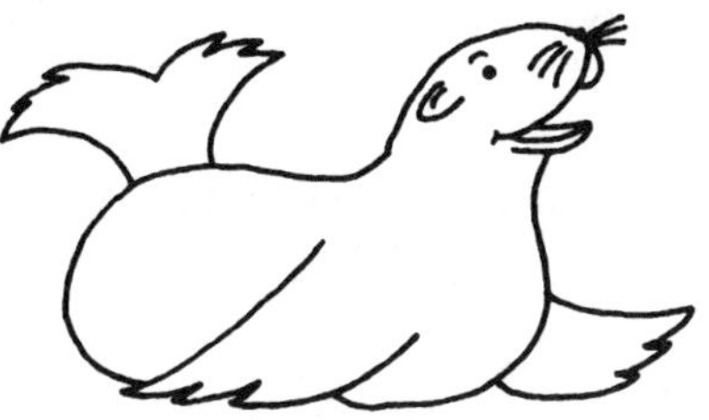

☞ When a writer makes all the changes in the rough draft, he or she writes the final copy of the **research report.**

Migrating Seals

Seals are migrating animals. Fur seals from the Pribilof Islands near Alaska migrate every fall.

Female and male fur seals migrate to different places. In the fall, female fur seals swim 3,000 miles to southern California. The male fur seals migrate to the Gulf of Alaska. They travel only 400 to 500 miles from their summer homes.

How to Write a Research Report

1. Write the title of your report.
2. Write the report. Use your rough draft.
3. Make all the changes you marked on your rough draft.
4. Indent the first sentence of each paragraph.

Practice

✎ On the lines below write some ideas of subjects you would like to research. Then take notes on one of the subjects. Write an outline and a rough draft. Then write a report.

____

____

____

____

____

Name ______________________ Date ____________

Unit Eight Assessment: Reading Comprehension

Read the story, then answer the questions.

While Madeline was in Holland, she had a strange adventure. Her first day there, she heard a windmill talking. "We have to be large," it said, "because we have important work to do." She was so surprised she ran into a shop that sold wooden shoes. The shoes spoke to her, too! Before Madeline left Holland, she spoke to a tulip, a bench, and a boat! She had quite a story to tell when she got home.

1. Where did Madeline go? ______________________
2. Why did the windmill surprise her?

   ____
3. Tell something in the story that could not really happen.

   ____
4. Tell something in the story that could have happened.

   ____
5. What did Madeline do right after the windmill surprised her? ______________________
6. What will probably happen when Madeline tells her story?

   ____
7. How could Madeline prove her story?

   ____
8. Would you believe her story? __________ Why or why not?

   ____

Name ______________________________ Date ______________

Drawing Conclusions

Hooray for Skunk!

Beaver talked his friend Skunk into going camping in the woods. Beaver had camped many times, but this would be Skunk's first camping trip. Beaver was an expert camper and told Skunk that he would set up their campsite.

Skunk tried to help, but he could not find anything that he could do right. Beaver cut down trees for shelter and for firewood. Then Skunk knocked over the stack of firewood. They went to catch fish for dinner, and Beaver caught a fish. Skunk only caught an old tin can. Skunk decided he was a terrible camper and wanted to stay only one night.

During the night, Beaver and Skunk woke up when they heard a loud noise. A fierce growl came from the bushes near the shelter. Beaver was terribly frightened. Skunk told Beaver not to worry and crawled out of the shelter. Skunk carefully walked toward the noise.

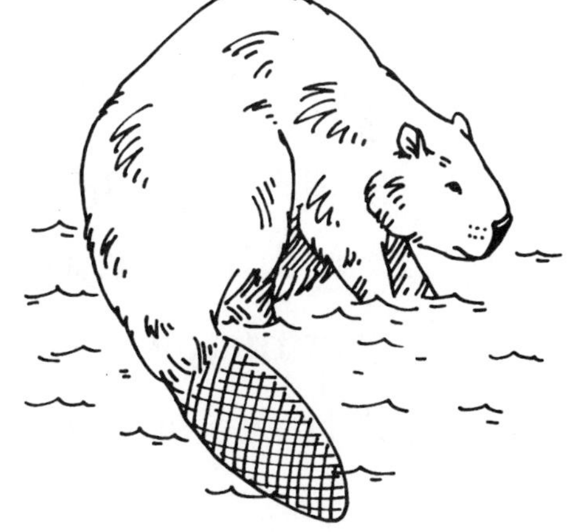

"Who is there?" asked Skunk.

"GROWL!" something answered.

Skunk quickly turned and sprayed the bushes with his horrible-smelling spray. Suddenly their friend Bear came out of the bushes coughing. Beaver and Skunk scolded Bear for scaring them. Beaver invited Skunk to go camping with him on every camping trip.

Skunk was pleased. "I might be a good camper after all," Skunk thought to himself as he fell asleep.

Go on to the next page.

Name ______________________________ Date ______________

Drawing Conclusions

Answer each question about the story. Circle the letter in front of the correct answer.

1. When things did not go well for Skunk, he probably felt
  a. as if he was a good camper.
  b. as if he was not helping Beaver.
  c. as if he wanted to go camping again soon.
  d. as if he wished he were camping alone.

2. Bear probably thought that his trick
  a. would make his friends run away.
  b. would scare the other forest animals.
  c. would make his friends laugh.
  d. would make his friends angry.

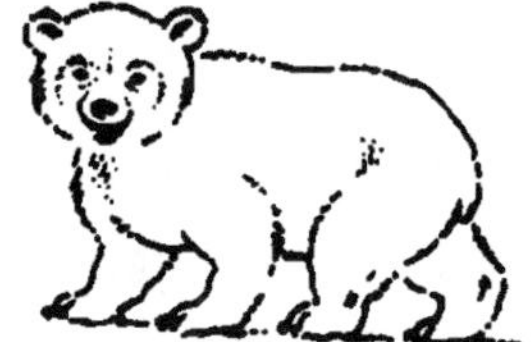

3. Bear will most likely
  a. try his trick again next time his friends go camping.
  b. try a different trick next time his friends go camping.
  c. bring his own spray the next time he tries his trick.
  d. not try to scare his friends again.

4. What does Beaver think about Skunk?
  a. Skunk is very brave.
  b. Skunk is a bad camper.
  c. Skunk is afraid of bears.
  d. Skunk knows how to fish.

Name ______________________ Date ______________

Comparing and Contrasting

Newton

Newton was a pig. He lived in a pigpen on a farm with many other pigs. Newton looked like the other pigs he knew. This made Newton feel plain and ordinary. Newton wanted to be special. He decided he needed to act differently from the other pigs to be special. So, when the rest of the pigs ate out of the trough, Newton put his food on a plate. When the other pigs relaxed in the mud, Newton would not get himself dirty.

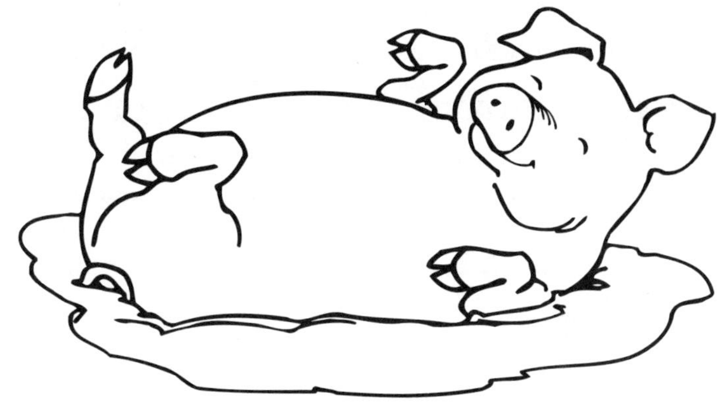

The other pigs did notice Newton, but not in the way that he wanted. Instead of thinking Newton was special, the other pigs made fun of him. They stopped playing with him.

One day Newton realized acting differently did not make him special. His friends had liked him before he started acting differently. So, Newton went back to his old ways, and soon all the pigs were playing with him again.

Go on to the next page.

Name ______________________ Date ____________

Comparing and Contrasting

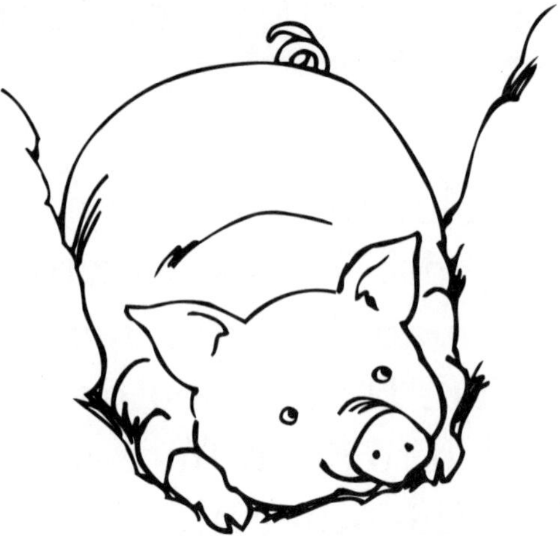

Answer each question about the story.

1. Name two ways in which Newton was different from the other pigs.

   a. ______________________

   b. ______________________

2. Name three ways in which Newton was the same as the other pigs.

   a. ______________________

   b. ______________________

   c. ______________________

3. Why did Newton want to be different from the other pigs?

   ____

   ____

4. Why did Newton start to act the same as the other pigs again?

   ____

   ____

Name ______________________________ Date ______________

Classifying Information

Beth Bee Is No Spider

Sarah Spider and Beth Bee were best friends. They lived in the same garden and had been friends since they were babies. Sarah was a very talented spider. Her mother had taught her how to spin the most beautiful webs. When she was spinning webs, she was as graceful as a ballerina. Friends often came to watch her spin because she made it look so easy. Artists often came to see the patterns she made in her webs. Sarah was unaware of all the attention. She just lived to spin webs. Her friend Beth was very proud of Sarah's skills. Sometimes, however, Beth felt sad because she did not think she could do anything as well as Sarah.

One day Beth decided to help Sarah spin a web. Beth touched a thread and she became trapped. When she tried to pull free, she tangled a thread around her wings. She ruined the web, and she felt terrible.

Sarah carefully set Beth free. Then they went to their favorite tomato plant to talk.

"How did you get trapped in my web?" Sarah asked. "You frightened me because you could have hurt yourself."

"I am so sorry," Beth cried. "I wanted to spin a web like you do. You spin webs so well, and I don't do anything well."

"There are many things that you could do," Sarah replied. "We will write a list. Then you can choose one thing, and we will find out how to do it!"

The two friends talked into the afternoon. They wrote a long list. Then Beth chose one new thing to learn how to do.

Go on to the next page.

Name ______________________________ Date ______________

Classifying Information

✏ Think about the story you read. Look at the diagram below. There are some ways that Sarah Spider and Beth Bee are alike. There are some ways that they are different. Add one item to each circle.

Remember, where the circles overlap shows how Beth and Sarah are alike.

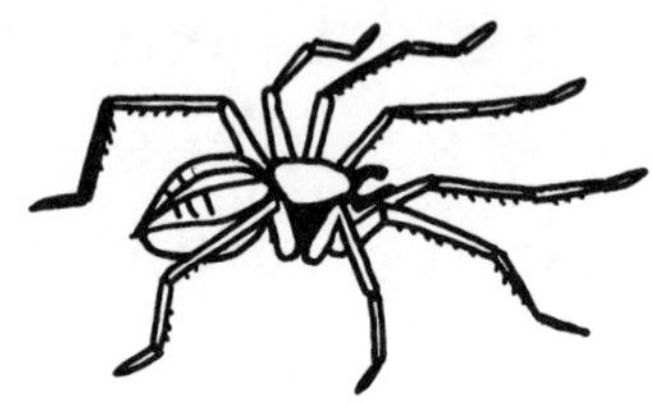

Sarah Spider	(overlap)	**Beth Bee**
1. Spins webs	1. Want to help each other	1. Makes honey
2. ______________	2. ______________	2. ______________

Name ______________________ Date ____________

Identifying Important Details

Kenny Saves the Day

Kenny looked forward to Thanksgiving Day every year. His grandpa always came to visit. Grandpa would share stories with Kenny, and they would laugh and talk for hours.

One year, after the family had eaten their Thanksgiving meal, Kenny's parents and his brother went to see a movie. Kenny and his grandpa thought about what they could do during the afternoon.

"I know," Kenny said. "Let's play football! I need a lot of practice."

"That sounds like fun," answered Grandpa. "Find the football, and I'll meet you in the yard."

Kenny and Grandpa passed the football back and forth many times. They practiced passing and catching. Suddenly, as Grandpa reached to catch a pass, he fell down.

"Grandpa, what's wrong?" asked Kenny.

"I stepped in a hole and tripped, Kenny," Grandpa answered slowly. "I think I broke my ankle. You will need to call for help."

Kenny hurried into the house to make the call. Beside the telephone he saw a list of telephone numbers. He carefully dialed the number next to the word *emergency*. A man's voice answered at the other end and asked Kenny several questions. Kenny answered each one.

An ambulance and Kenny's parents arrived at almost the same time. Kenny could see that Grandpa was in good hands.

"We are glad that you were here to help Grandpa," Kenny's parents said. "We are proud of you for taking such good care of him."

Go on to the next page.

Name ______________________________ Date ______________

Identifying Important Details

Answer each question about the story. Circle the letter in front of the correct answer.

1. Why does Kenny like Thanksgiving Day?
   a. He enjoys all the food.
   b. He likes to watch football.
   c. He spends time with Grandpa.
   d. He reads stories.

2. What do Kenny and his grandpa decide to do?
   a. play football
   b. go to a movie
   c. eat again
   d. talk

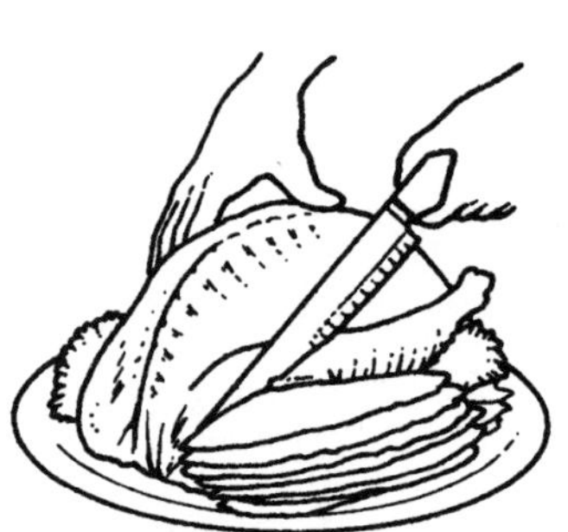

3. How does Kenny's grandpa help Kenny?
   a. Grandpa cooks the Thanksgiving meal.
   b. Grandpa feeds Kenny.
   c. Grandpa helps Kenny practice football.
   d. Grandpa throws the football too far.

4. How does Kenny help Grandpa?
   a. He calls for help.
   b. He listens to Grandpa.
   c. He asks the neighbors for help.
   d. He calls his parents.

Name ______________________________ Date ______________

Sequencing

A Mountain Hike

Nancy and her father planned to hike up a mountain trail. The trail they chose was long and led to the top of a mountain. She and her father had packed a picnic lunch earlier in the morning. They both carried backpacks and a few other supplies.

As they started up the trail, Nancy's father pointed out the many different flowers and trees. He showed Nancy the difference between the leaves of an oak tree and a maple tree. Soon, Nancy was pointing out different kinds of trees to her father.

"Look over there," Nancy whispered suddenly. They had just turned a corner of the trail. To the side of the path was a tiny baby raccoon. It appeared to be lost as it stumbled around in the tall grass.

"Its mother must be close by. Do you think we should stop here and watch it?" she asked.

"That's a good idea," her father answered. "We can eat our lunch while we watch the baby raccoon."

Nancy and her father sat beside the trail and ate their lunch. They watched the tiny raccoon until it tired itself out and fell asleep. Soon, a larger raccoon came through the bushes and sat down next to the baby raccoon.

Nancy and her father packed up their supplies and continued up the mountain. They knew the tiny raccoon was safe.

Go on to the next page.

Name ______________________ Date ______________

Sequencing

Answer each question about the story. Circle the letter in front of the correct answer.

1. What had Nancy and her father done earlier in the morning?
   a. They had chosen a trail.
   b. They had pointed out different trees.
   c. They had seen a baby raccoon.
   d. They had packed a picnic lunch.

2. What did Nancy do just after they turned a corner of the trail?
   a. She saw a baby raccoon.
   b. She pointed out different types of trees.
   c. She ate her lunch.
   d. She took a nap.

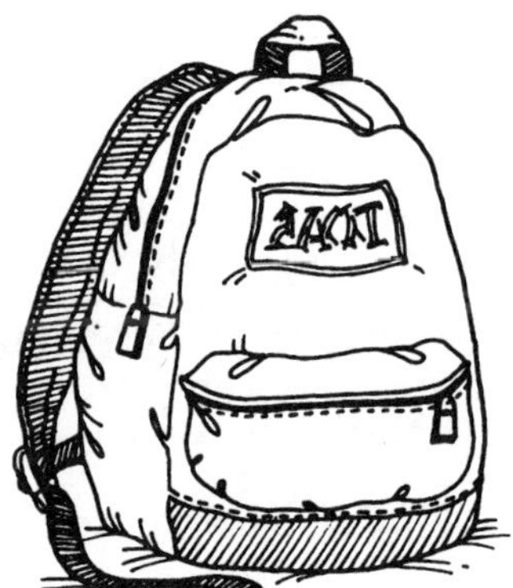

3. What did Nancy and her father do before the mother raccoon came?
   a. They packed up their supplies and continued up the mountain.
   b. They played with the baby raccoon.
   c. They sat beside the trail and ate their lunch.
   d. They trapped the baby raccoon.

4. What did the baby raccoon do after it tired itself out?
   a. It followed Nancy and her father.
   b. It looked for its mother.
   c. It fell asleep.
   d. It got lost.

Name ______________________________ Date ______________

Identifying Cause and Effect

The Candlemaker

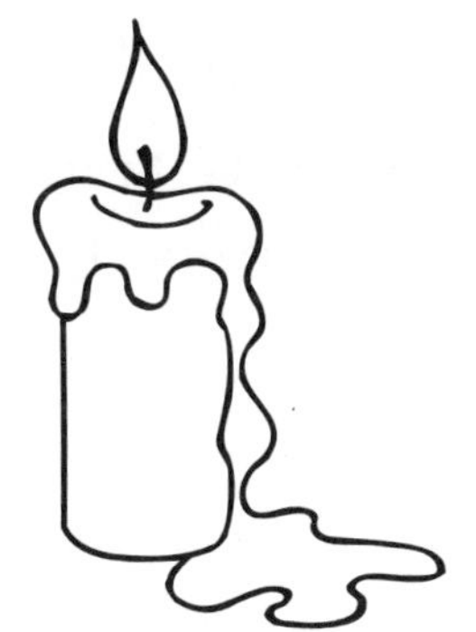

There once was a candlemaker from Brighton who made wonderful candles of all colors, shapes, and sizes. People came from near and far to admire and buy his candles. The candlemaker enjoyed making his candles so much that it did not seem right to ask people to pay for them. He gave candles away until there were none left to give.

One day, he reached into his cupboard for more dye, and there was none. He searched for more tallow, and there was none. He found string for the wick. However, without tallow or dye he could not make any candles. He had given away his last candle, and he did not know what to do.

He went to see his friend the woodcutter.

"I have no candles to give to the people," he said. "You will need to work very hard to chop wood today. People will depend on the light from their fireplaces." It was soon known throughout the country that there were no more beautiful candles in Brighton.

That evening, neighbors arrived with the woodcutter. They brought tallow and dye for the candlemaker. He was surprised and pleased. The candlemaker asked them why they had brought supplies.

"You have been giving us candles for years," answered the woodcutter. "Brighton would no longer be bright if you stopped making candles."

Go on to the next page.

Name ______________________ Date ______________

Identifying Cause and Effect

Finish each sentence about the story. Circle the *cause* in each sentence. Underline the *effect*.

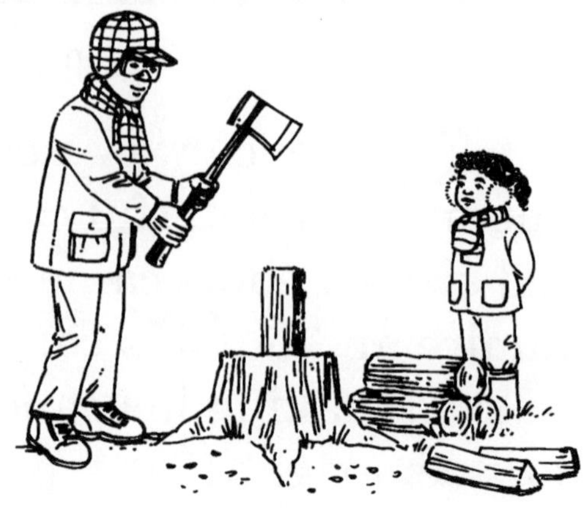

1. People came from near and far because

____

____

2. The candlemaker gave his candles away because

____

____

3. The candlemaker went to see the woodcutter because

____

____

4. Because the people wanted the candlemaker to keep making candles, they ______________________________

____

5. Because the people brought more tallow and dye, the candlemaker ______________________________

____

Name ______________________________ Date ______________

Making Judgments

A Surprise in the Forest

Zach and Wendy went with their parents to the meadow for a picnic. After the picnic, Zach and Wendy wandered close to the forest to see the wildflowers growing there. Suddenly, a deer leaped out from behind a tree and stopped to look at them. When the deer ran back into the forest, Zach and Wendy followed it.

The deer ran straight down a well-worn path. It was not hard to follow the deer at first, but then the deer turned off the path and disappeared among the trees. Zach and Wendy could not see where the deer had gone, so they decided to return to the meadow.

Just then a bear stood up on the path close to them. Zach and Wendy stood very still, hoping the bear would go away. The bear did not move either. After a long minute, Zach grabbed Wendy's hand and started running down the path. They thought they heard the bear behind them, but when they turned around the bear was not there.

Zach and Wendy ran the rest of the way to the meadow. They shared their adventure with their parents. Both the children decided that deer looked best in a safe, open field.

Go on to the next page.

Name ______________________ Date ____________

Making Judgments

Answer each question about the story.

1. Should the children have gone close to the forest? __________

   Why or why not? ______________________________

   ____

2. Do you think Zach and Wendy should have followed the deer? __________

   Why or why not? ______________________________

   ____

3. Should Zach and Wendy have run from the bear? __________

   Why or why not? ______________________________

   ____

4. What would you have done if you had seen the bear?

   ____

   ____

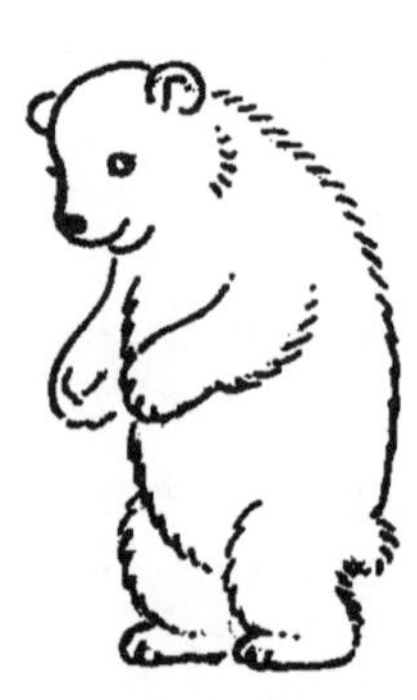

Name ______________________________ Date ______________

Summarizing

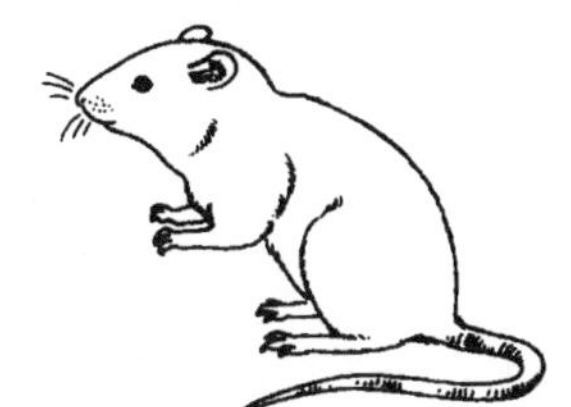

Lucky Milly

Milly the mouse poked her head out of her mouse hole. She carefully looked all around the kitchen, watching for Jep the cat. Jep was nowhere to be seen.

"Good!" Milly thought. "Now is a good time to eat the Swiss cheese on the kitchen table."

Milly scurried across the kitchen floor. Just as she reached the leg of the table, Jep crawled out from behind the washing machine where he had been hiding. Jep slowly moved closer to Milly. Milly looked all around the kitchen for a way to escape. From where she was, there was no way to reach her mouse hole. Not knowing what else to do, Milly scampered up the table leg just as Jep pounced. She dove into one of the holes in the cheese as Jep landed on the table. He looked all over the table and the kitchen, but he could not find her. Jep knew she had not made it back to her mouse hole, so he decided to go back to his bed and wait for her. As Jep sat waiting for Milly to come out of hiding, he became tired and soon fell fast asleep.

Meanwhile, Milly was still in the Swiss cheese greedily nibbling all she could eat. When she had eaten her fill, she poked her head out of the cheese and looked for Jep. She saw him sleeping soundly in his bed. Milly crawled back down to her mouse hole, a very happy mouse.

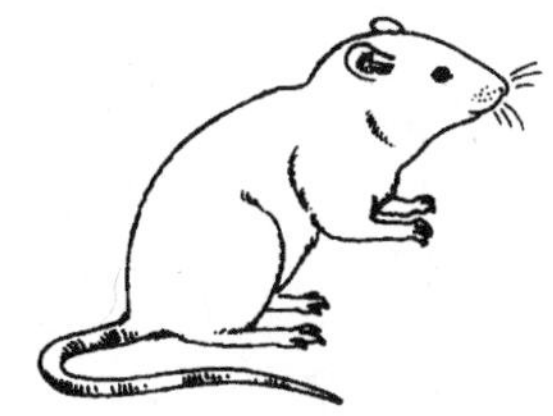

Go on to the next page.

Name ______________________________ Date ________________

Summarizing

Think about the story you read. Write four or five sentences that summarize the story. Remember, a summary does not tell all the details, but tells the main points of the story.

Name ______________________________ Date ______________

What Will Happen Next?

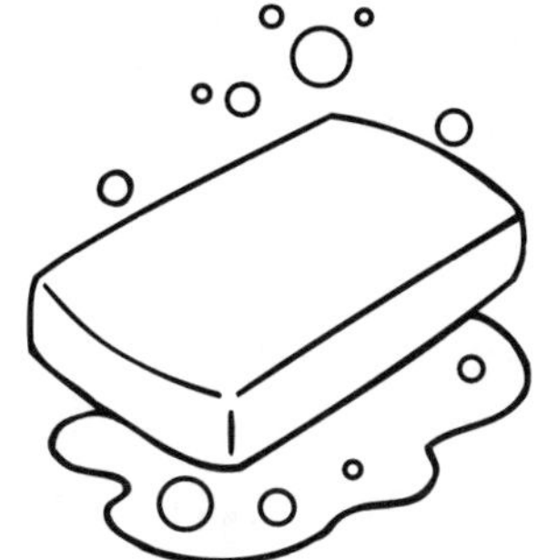

Read each paragraph. Then answer the questions. Circle the letter in front of the correct answer.

Kiley Riley hurried to check the mail. She found a box addressed to her. It said *Secret Soap*. She read the directions, which said, "Wash evenly to disappear. Use again to reappear." Kiley took the soap into the bathroom.

1. What will Kiley do next?

a. She will take a bath with her regular soap.

b. She will brush her teeth.

c. She will use the secret soap and disappear.

d. She will use her regular soap and disappear.

Kiley and her clothes were completely invisible. She went to school, but no one could see her. Eric Clark almost ran over her with his bicycle. The crossing guard did not see her, and she was almost hit by a car. The teacher shut the door in her face. Kiley did not like being invisible. She went home and hurried into the bathroom.

2. What will Kiley do next?

a. She will use the soap to reappear.

b. She will get her bike and run into Eric.

c. She will send the soap back to the company that made it.

d. She will stay invisible a while longer.

Go on to the next page.

Name ______________________ Date ______________

What Will Happen Next?

Read each paragraph. Then answer the questions. Circle the letter in front of the correct answer.

The children looked out the window at the brightly colored leaves on the ground. Jenny, Paul, and Mike rushed outside to rake the leaves into a large pile. Then the children moved away from the pile and got ready to run.

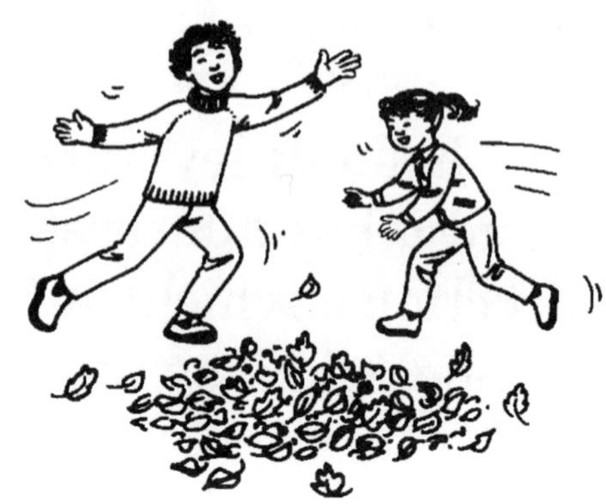

3. What will the children do next?

a. They will put the leaves into bags.

b. They will run and jump into the pile of leaves.

c. They will play a game of baseball.

d. They will go into the house.

The children jumped into the leaves until the pile was scattered all around the yard. They brushed the leaves off their clothes and out of their hair. Then they went and picked up their rakes again. They walked to where the leaves were spread around the ground.

4. What will the children do next?

a. They will put the rakes away.

b. They will go inside and rest.

c. They will rake the leaves again.

d. They will jump into the scattered leaves.

Name ______________________________ Date ______________

What's the Main Idea?

Read each paragraph. Choose the answer that tells the main idea of each paragraph. Circle the letter in front of the correct answer.

Lana and her family were preparing for their summer vacation. They were going to the lake. They were packing the car. They packed clothes, books, and games for rainy days. Soon the car was full of their things.

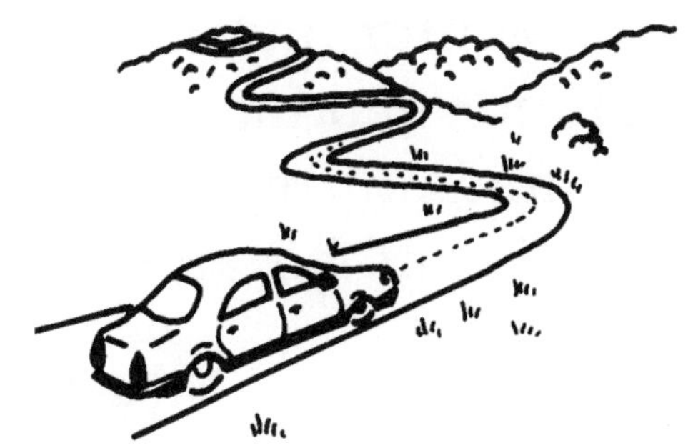

1. What is the main idea of this paragraph?

a. Lana and her family were packing the car.

b. They packed clothes, books, and games.

c. Soon the car was full of their things.

d. Lana and her family were preparing for their summer vacation.

They were visiting Lana's aunt. The cottage was in the woods by the lake. There were trees all around the cottage. There were birds in the trees. Small animals lived in the woods, too.

2. What is the main idea of this paragraph?

a. Small animals lived in the woods.

b. The cottage was in the woods by the lake.

c. There were trees all around the cottage.

d. There were birds in the trees.

Go on to the next page.

Name ______________________ Date ______________

What's the Main Idea?

Read each paragraph. Choose the answer that tells the main idea of each paragraph. Circle the letter in front of the correct answer.

Winter had come almost overnight. The new snow was just right for making a snowman. Sam put on his snow pants, coat, hat, and mittens. He got a carrot and some raisins. Sam went outside and began to roll the snow into large balls.

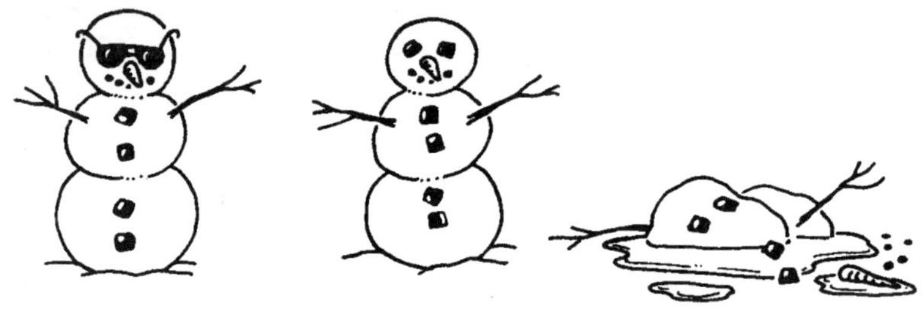

3. What is the main idea of this paragraph?

a. Winter had come almost overnight.

b. Sam put on his snow pants, coat, hat, and mittens.

c. The new snow was just right for making a snowman.

d. He got a carrot and some raisins.

The next day was very warm, and the snow began to melt. The snowman got smaller and smaller. First, his nose fell off. Then, his arms fell out. Finally, the snowman's body disappeared into a puddle of water.

4. What is the main idea of this paragraph?

a. The snowman's body disappeared.

b. First, his nose fell off.

c. Then, his arms fell out.

d. The day was very warm, and the snow began to melt.

Name ______________________________ Date ______________

Finding the Main Idea

Read each paragraph. Then write the sentence from the paragraph that tells the main idea.

Howard was a very shy little turtle. He was afraid to talk to anyone. He would always hide in his shell when new turtles came around. He pulled in his head and legs. He spent a lot of time inside his shell!

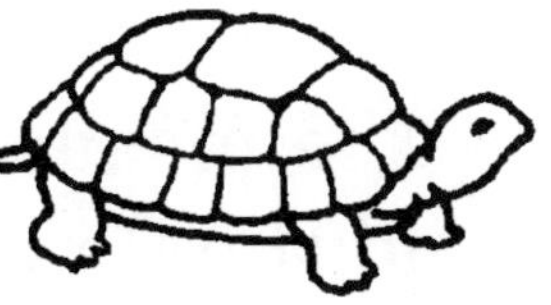

1. What is the sentence that tells the main idea of this paragraph?

____

____

____

Howard's mother tried to help Howard. She took him places where they would meet new turtles. She tried to get him used to new faces. She made him say hello to other turtles. Howard's mother was determined to make him less shy.

2. What is the sentence that tells the main idea of this paragraph?

____

____

____

Go on to the next page.

Name ______________________ Date ____________

Finding the Main Idea.

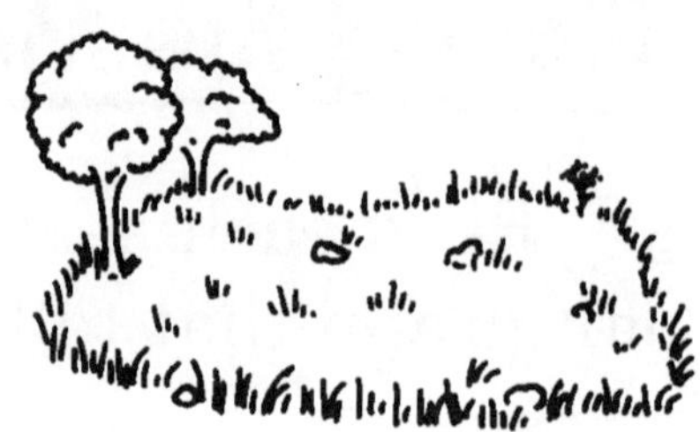

Read each paragraph. Then write the sentence from the paragraph that tells the main idea.

The meadow is full of all kinds of animal life. Insects buzz around the flowers. Little rabbits hop among the tall grass. Mice and moles make their homes here.

3. What is the sentence that tells the main idea of this paragraph?

____

____

____

Judy likes the meadow. In spring it is full of new life and the smell of new grass. In summer it is full of life and pretty flowers. In the fall, the meadow is surrounded by trees of all colors. In the winter, the meadow is a great place for walking. Judy loves to come to the meadow in all the seasons.

4. What is the sentence that tells the main idea of this paragraph?

____

____

____

Name ______________________________ Date ______________

Say It Your Way

Read each paragraph. Then write, in your own words, a sentence that tells what the paragraph is about.

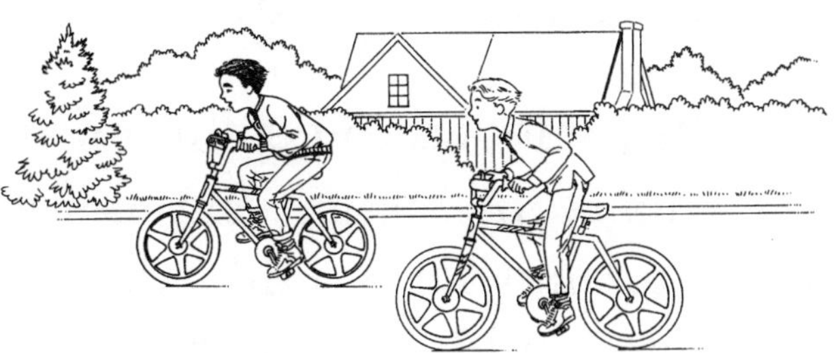

John had wanted a new bicycle for his birthday, and now he had it! It was exactly the one he had seen in the store so many times. He had admired its color and its smooth ride. John was as happy as he could be as he hopped on and rode his new bicycle down the street.

1. In your own words, what is this paragraph about?

____

____

____

John's best friend had gotten a new bike on his birthday, too. Together they raced around the blocks of their neighborhood, waving to their friends as they passed. They rode their new bikes all afternoon until it was time to go in for dinner.

2. In your own words, what is this paragraph about?

____

____

____

Go on to the next page.

Name ______________________ Date ____________

Say It Your Way

Read each paragraph. Then write, in your own words, a sentence that tells what the paragraph is about.

Ginny loved to go shopping. The best time was right before school started each year. Her mother would take her to the mall, and they would shop all day. They had lunch at the food court. Ginny loved having her mother to herself all day, and she loved having new things to wear to school.

3. In your own words, what is this paragraph about?

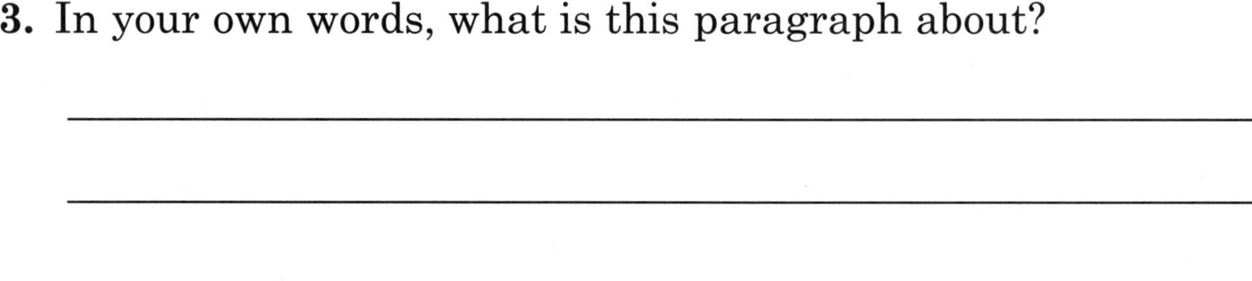

This year, Ginny's little sister was starting school, too. She came with Ginny and her mother when they went shopping. Ginny didn't want to share her day with her little sister at first. But her sister looked so cute in her new clothes that Ginny decided she didn't mind after all.

4. In your own words, what is this paragraph about?

____

____

____

Name ______________________________ Date ______________

Reality or Fantasy?

Anything Man

There once was a man who could turn himself into any shape he wanted. Once he locked himself out of his house, and so he turned himself into a key and unlocked his door. Another time he turned into the shape of an airplane and flew around the world.

One day, a little girl ran up to him, crying, “Oh, help me! My kitten is stuck in the drainpi e!”

The man told the girl he would rescue the kitten. The girl led him to the drainpipe. Then the man changed himself into the shape of a spring. He crawled into the pipe and told the girl to pull on his legs and then let go. She followed his directions exactly. The man sprang through the pipe, grabbed the kitten, and came out the other side.

The man quickly changed back to himself and gave the kitten to the girl. She thanked him and took her kitten home. Dusting himself off, the man continued walking down the street.

Go on to the next page.

Name ______________________________ Date ______________

Reality or Fantasy?

Read each sentence from the story. Write whether the sentence is real or fantasy. Write *R* if the sentence tells about something that could really happen. Write *F* if the sentence tells about something that is fantasy and could not really happen.

1. The man could turn himself into anything. ______
2. Once he turned himself into a key. ______
3. Another time he turned himself into a plane. ______
4. One day a little girl was crying. ______
5. She asked the man for help. ______
6. Her kitten was stuck in a drainpipe. ______
7. The man changed into a spring. ______
8. He reached into the pipe and grabbed the kitten. ______
9. When the girl let go of his legs, he sprang through the pipe with the kitten. ______
10. The man changed back into his regular form. ______
11. The girl thanked him and took her kitten home. ______
12. The man dusted himself off and walked down the street. ______

Name ______________________ Date ____________

Problems and Solutions

Sweater Weather

Once there was a kind woman named Mrs. McCan who lived all alone in a small cottage. The cottage had only a fireplace to heat it. Every winter Mrs. McCan bought wood for the fireplace and stayed nice and warm.

One winter there was no wood left to buy. Mrs. McCan did not know how she could stay warm. Mrs. McCan sat down to think about what she should do. While she thought, she began to knit a sweater. For many days Mrs. McCan sat and thought, knitting the entire time.

She stopped knitting one day and looked at the sweater. It was as big as the room.

"This is the answer!" Mrs. McCan said excitedly. She decided to knit a sweater for the cottage. Mrs. McCan measured the cottage and finished the sweater the next day.

To this day, every winter, Mrs. McCan wraps a large, warm sweater around the cottage. She stays warm and cozy all winter.

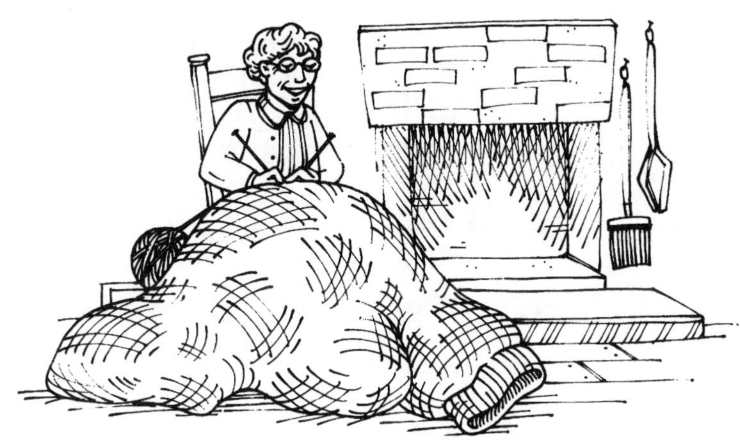

Go on to the next page.

Name ______________________ Date ______________

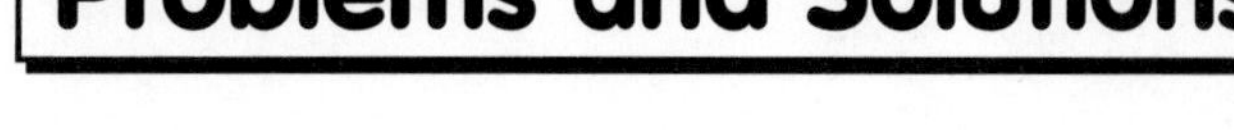

Problems and Solutions

Answer each question about the story.

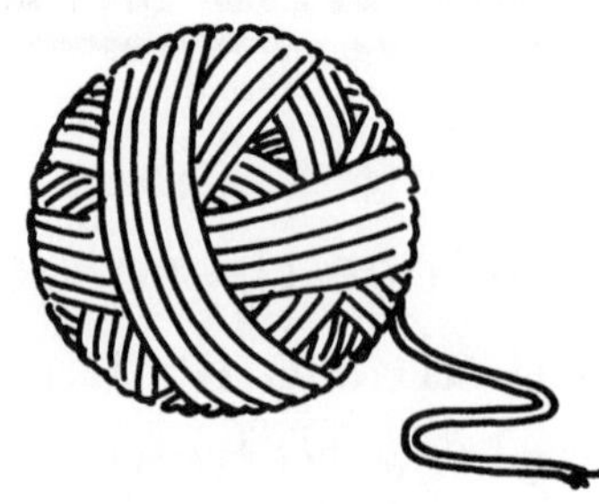

1. What was Mrs. McCan's problem?

____

____

2. How did Mrs. McCan usually heat her cottage?

____

____

3. Why did Mrs. McCan have to find a new way to heat her cottage?

____

____

4. What is Mrs. McCan's solution to her problem?

____

____

5. Do you think Mrs. McCan's solution could really work? ____ Why or why not?

____

____

Language Arts Handbook
Grade Three
Answer Key

P. 5 Unit One Assessment: 1. proper noun, 2. common noun 3. pronoun, 4. adjective, 5. past tense verb, 6. possessive noun, 7. contraction, 8. compound word, 9. plural noun, 10. present tense verb, 11. circle is, 12. came, 13. went, 14. ate, 15. began, 16. thought, 17. said, 18. took, 19. rang, 20. met

P. 6 1. Many fruits grow in the United States., 2. Many vegetables are grown in this country, too., 3. Much rice is grown in China., 4. Did you know that raisins are made from grapes?, 6. Prunes are really dried plums., 6. There is a plant called a fern., 7. Much heather grows in the hills of Scotland., 8. Some cucumbers are used to make pickles., 9. Different potatoes are grown in Idaho and Ireland., 10. Large mangos are grown in Mexico., 11. A fruit grown in Hawaii is the pineapple., 12. In Indiana, corn and beans are grown.

P. 7 1. Indians, 2. trail, 3. hedgehog, 4. cacti, 5. spines, 6. branches 7. bunches, 8. bush, 9. eggs, 10. men

P. 8 1. friends, 2. ranches, 3. stories, 4. dresses, 5. stitches 6. brooches, 7. deer, 8. Stores

P. 9 1. shop's, 2. bowls', 3. family's, 4. wall's, 5. voices', 6. Lana's

P. 10 1. child's, 2. friends', 3. dad's, 4. shop's, 5. hamsters', 6. animal's, 7. creature's, 8. family's, 9. Father's, 10. cage's

P. 11 11 Answers may vary. Suggested answers: 1. made, 2. started 3. tested, 4. squeezed, 5. zoomed, 6. shouted, 7. hit, flipped 8. brushed, 9. thought, 10. added, 11. raced, 12. stopped

P. 12 1. crossed, 2. visited, 3. finished, 4. hangs, 5. knows, 6. waited

P. 13 1. shaped, 2. hummed, 3. moved, 4. tried, 5. changed, 6. planned, 7. hurried, 8. used, 9. supplied, 10. stopped

P. 14 1. am, 2. were, 3. are, 4. was, 5. was, 6. were, 7. was, 8. are 9. am

P. 15 1. have, 2. has, 3. can, 4. have, 5. can, 6. can, 7. can, 8. have 9. have, 10. has, 11. have, 12. has

P. 16 1. come, 2. came, 3. came, 4. comes, 5. came, 6. come

P. 17 1. go, 2. went, 3. gone, 4. went, 5. gone, 6. went, 7. gone, 8. went

P. 18 1. begun, 2. sing, 3. kept, 4. says, 5. thought, 6. given

P. 19 1. rung, 2. took, 3. said, 4. eat, 5. ran, 6. keeps, 7. met

P. 20 1. hundred, 2. soft, 3. many, 4. reddish, 5. the, 6. A, 7. white

P. 21 1. cooler, 2. hardest, 3. most important, 4. more comfortable

P. 22 1. larger, 2. thicker, 3. thinner, 4. cutest, 5. strongest

P. 23 1. It, 2. He, 3. She, 4. it, 5. They, 6. We, 7. She

P. 24 1. They, 2. he, 3. We, 4. her, 5. They

P. 25 A. Answers may vary. Suggested answers: treehouse, ladybug, someday, afternoon, doghouse, underground, flashlight, schoolteacher, countryside, B. 1. herself, 2. itself, 3. inside 4. doghouse, 5. bedroom, 6. afternoon, 7. underground

P. 26 1. hadn't, 2. they're, 3. hasn't, 4. She's, 5. You're, 6. I'm 7. haven't, 8. It's, 9. weren't, 10. wasn't, 11. isn't, 12. It's, 13. We're

P. 27 Unit Two Assessment: 1-2, answers will vary. Examples: 1. takes long walks, 2. My dog, 3. exclamation, 4. asking, 5. telling, 6. command, 7. Robins and cardinals sing a pretty song., 8. Bears hibernate and stay warm in the winter., 9. We were looking for a book and my sister found it for me., 10. The flowers are bright, pretty, and colorful., 11. Answers will vary. Examples: wild, brown, young

P. 28 Answers will vary. Examples: 1. are friends, 2. felt good 3. Manny, 4. Tony, 5. jumped, 6. formed, 7. were angry 8. The crab

P. 29 1. ?, 2. ., 3. ?, 4. ., 5. ?, 6. ., 7. ?, 8. ., 9. ., 10. ., 11. ?, 12. .

P. 30 1. !, 2. ., 3. !, 4. !, 5. !, 6. ., 7. ., 8. ., 9. !, 10. ., 11. ., 12. !

P. 31 1. Robins and cardinals sing in spring., 2. Animals and insects awake from a long winter's sleep., 3. The animals and birds are active in summer., 4. Snakes and toads hibernate in winter.

P. 32 1. Daniel mounted his scooter and went to the library., 2. The librarian saw Daniel and asked if he needed help., 3. Daniel took the book and checked it out., 4. Mama stopped cooking and looked at the book Daniel had gotten.

P. 33 1. The rocky cliffs are steep and bare., 2. The summer sky is clear, blue, and beautiful., 3. The flowers in the field are pretty, yellow, and tall., 4. The alfalfa smells sweet and fresh.

P. 34 1. Explorers followed rivers, and they used the rivers like roads. 2. Loggers cut down trees, and the trees floated down the river., 3. Indians used clay for pottery, and sometimes they used clay for bricks., 4. The river is beautiful, and it is also useful., 5. Settlers looked for the right place, and they built new homes., 6. More and more people settled in America, and the river towns grew.

P. 35 Answers will vary. Possible answers: 1. bragged, 2. tricked 3. demanded, 4. ran, 5. searched, 6. strolled, 7. called

P. 36 Answers will vary. Possible answers: 1. green, thick, 2. sweet 3. blue, 4. summer, 5. soft, 6. warm, 7. buzzing, 8. cool 9. wonderful

P. 37 1. Today we read about spiders., 2. Last year I had read about spiders., 3. Then the teacher showed pictures of spiders., 4. At night, some spiders spin webs. 5. Yesterday I saw a spider in the garden., 6. Tomorrow I will bring my spider poster.

P. 38 Unit Three Assessment: 1. big, 2. searched, 3. enjoy, 4. never 5. cried, 6. hard, 7. circle, 8. circle, 9. no circle, 10. circle 11. circle, 12. circle, 13. circle, 14. no circle, 15. circle, 16. two 17. eye, 18. ate, 19. I, 20. me, 21. enjoy, 22. looks

P. 39 1. scared, 2. quiet, 3. coming, 4. shake, 5. discovered 6. searched, 7. difficult, 8. saved, 9. began, 10. enjoyed

P. 40 1. started, 2. hard, 3. true, 4. always, 5. cried, 6. Before, 7. ended 8. never, 9. under, 10. something, 11. easy, 12. fast

P. 41 1. unusual, 2. impatient, 3. disliked, 4. unlucky, 5. impossible 6. unlike, 7. retraced, 8. reappeared

P. 42 1. aviator, 2. inventor, 3. useful, 4. helper, 5. fearless, 6. joyful 7. successful, 8. harmless

P. 43 Answers will vary. Examples: 1. She doesn't have the will to stop eating chocolate., 2. The meat was lean., 3. I wound the thread around my finger., 4. Pencils do not have lead anymore., 5. The water won't last long., 6. Don't tear that paper!, 7. A bat is flying near the light.

P. 44 1. pair, 2. sun, 3. they're, 4. knows, 5. so, 6. One, 7. see 8. There, 9. hear, 10. made, 11. for, 12. here, 13. hour, 14. would 15. eye, 16. blue, 17. ate, 18. know

P. 45 1. St., 2. IL., 3. Mon., Aug., 4. Mr., 5. Rd., 6. IN, 7. Fri., Feb.

P. 46 1. to, 2. too, 3. two, 4. to, 5. Two, 6. to, 7. There, 8. there, 9. their 10. They're, 11. There, 12. They're

P. 47 1. You're, 2. your, 3. your, 4. You're, 5. your, 6. its, 7. It's, 8. its 9. It's, 10. It's, 11. it's, 12. your

P. 48 1. I, 2. me, 3. I, 4. I, 5. I, 6. me, 7. I, 8. I, 9. I, 10. me

P. 49 1. strolls, 2. watches, 3. enjoys, 4. pass, 5. sees, 6. touch 7. takes, 8. fill, 9. teaches, 10. understands

P. 50 Unit Four Assessment: 1. "Where are you going?" asked Mrs. Brown., 2. "I need to find my glasses," answered Mr. Brown. 3. We are going to be late if you don't hurry!, 4. We should arrive by 1:30 P.M., 5. Where did you see them last?, 6. They were on the book called The Old West., There is a poem called "The Old West," too., 8. That's a fantastic poem!, 9. First, we are going to Topeka, Kansas., 10. The date was April 7, 1995., 11. My brother Jimmy was born in Washington on the Fourth of July., 12. I live in the state of Massachusetts in the United States., 13. Barnaby is reading a book called In the Saddle.

P. 51 Words to be capitalized listed only: 1. Samantha Star 2. Ed Endive, 3. Mr., 4. Ms., 5. Dr., 6. J. R., 7. T. C., 8. G. 9. I, 10. I

P. 52 Words to be capitalized listed only: 1. Bologna, Italy, 2. Cherry Hill, New Jersey, 3. Lyme, Connecticut, 4. Boise, Idaho, 5. Dover, Delaware, 6. Forest Avenue, 7. Larkspur Lane, 8. Squash Blvd., 9. Walnut Hill, 10. Turnip Street, 11. Green Road, 12. Strawberry Lane

P. 53 Words to be capitalized listed only: 1. Monday, October 2. Wednesday, 3. Friday, 4. October, 5. November, 6. Columbus Day, 7. Halloween, 8. Thanksgiving Day

P. 54 1. Tony and Manny are best friends., 2. They have been friends for a long time., 3. They play baseball., 4. Sometimes they go fishing., 5. Is there a snake in the poem "That's Me"?, 6. You will enjoy reading the book Beautiful Bugs and Other Creatures.

P. 55 1. Manny and Tony go to the beach every day., 2. They take a picnic lunch., 3. Do not step on the crabs., 4. Dr. Quick looked at Mr. Smith's toe., 5. Mrs. Smith found a bandage., 6. Dr. Quick helped Mr. Smith., 7. Period after each Roman numeral.

P. 56 1. ?, 2. ?, 3. ?, 4. ?, 5. ?, 6. ?, 7. ?, 8. !, 9. !, 10. !, 11. ?, 12. ! 13. !, 14. !

P. 57 Commas needed after New Delhi, July 27, Chandra, and Sincerely.

P. 58 1. First, we looked for food by the river., 2. Next, we looked in every cave., 3. Then, we returned home., 4. First, we said we would like some wild berries., 5. Then, we thought of a plan. 6. Finally, we told the others our idea., 7. We decided to go fishing, and we went to the lake., 8. We brought our fishing poles, and we brought some bait., 9. We dug a pit, and we started a fire. 10. We got the fish ready, and we cooked them for dinner.

P. 59 1. Meghan and her family took the 8:30 P.M. train., 2. At 7:15 the next morning, they ate breakfast., 3. The train pulled into Union Station at 8:45 A.M., 4. Meghan didn't want to waste time. 5. She wasn't interested in looking at the city from their windows. 6. Meghan's cousins met them at the hotel., 7. Her cousins' rooms overlooked the lake., 8. Meghan's father took them to the fair.

P. 60 1. Find out more about wind power in the book Catch the Wind. 2. Wind power and other kinds of energy are explained in the book Energy All Around., 3. The book Silent Friend, Silent Foe tells about the power of the wind., 4. I need to return the book Storm Track to the library., 5. "Who Has Seen the Wind?" is a lovely poem., 6. "Ten-Dollar Wind" is a story about a lost ten-dollar bill., 7. The story "Something in the Wind" is a mystery. 8. I can hear bells ringing when I read the poem "Wind Chimes."

P. 61 Unit Five Assessment: Writing will vary. Students should write complete sentences, well-written paragraphs, and follow other requirements of writing type chosen.

P. 62 Answers will vary. Students should think of a workable solution to the problem.

P. 63 Answers will vary. Possible answers: Title: Hoppy Frog, The cool water comes down, Will the little frog drown?, Possible Second Verse: Hoppy jumped high. He jumped out of the deep sink. He didn't want a cool bath. He only wanted a drink!

P. 64 News articles will vary. Students should write a headline, an introductory sentence, and tell who, what, when, and where.

P. 65 Possible words for chart: canoes, boots, trees, under rocks, tents, woodpiles, backpacks

P. 66 Sentences will vary.

P. 67 Sentences will vary.

P. 68 Reasons will vary. Possible answers: 1. thank-you for a gift 2. thank-you for hospitality, 3. thank-you for help of some kind

P. 69 Addresses will vary, but should follow correct form as shown.

P. 70 Journal entries will vary, but should include date and some details about what happened and how student felt.

P. 71 Book reports will vary, but must include title, author, summary, and opinion.

P. 72 Paragraphs will vary, but should include topic sentence with main idea and good supporting sentences with details.

P. 73 Some hunters use their teeth to catch food., Others run to trap food., Some jump on insects to catch them.

P. 74 1. Get a rubber band and a jar with holes in the lid., 2. Sneak up on the fly slowly., 3. Put the rubber band over the index finger of one hand. With your other hand, pull back the rubber band. 5. Aim and let go., 6. Put the fly in the jar.

P. 75 1. They both migrate thousands of miles., 2. They travel in large groups to reach warmer weather.

P. 76 1. Arctic terns fly mainly over water., 2. Bobolinks fly mostly over land., 3. Arctic terns dive into the water to feed on fish. 4. Bobolinks hunt on land for insects and grain.

P. 77 What Happened: Indians lived near rivers., Why It Happened: drinking water, food, rich soil for crops

P. 78 saving lives, protecting homes, protecting food supplies

P. 79 interesting, desert, special, large, heavy, hot

P. 80 Feelings: father was thoughtless; Reasons: he lied about his daughter, he did not think about what would happen

P. 81 Feeling: dog should be replaced with woofer; Reasons: dog has nothing to do with the way a dog looks, acts, or sounds

P. 82 Paragraphs will vary, but should tell about incident in student's life and include at least three sentences.

P. 83 Unit Seven Assessment: 1. Art Projects at the Beach, 2. 32 3. 8 and 10-30, 4. nonfiction, 5. fiction, 6. cherry and chip 7. yes; Animal paragraphs will vary. Students should show notes and write a paragraph with topic sentence and supporting details. Paragraph should be in student's own words.

P. 84 1. Art Projects at the Beach, 2. Sandy Shore, 3. Crafts Books, Inc., 4. Getting Started, 5. 8-10, 26, 29

P. 85 1. nonfiction, 2. nonfiction, 3. nonfiction, 4. fiction, 5. s, 6. p, 7. w 8. i, 9. b, 10. f

P. 86 A. 1., B. 4. to open, 5. octo

P. 87 1. chip, because it is the second guide word, 2. carrot, cactus 3. no

P. 88 1. clover, 2, 2. beet, 1, 3. pickle, 2, 4. pear, 1, 5. wheat, 1

P. 89 1. 5, 2. 3, 3. 1, 4. pronunciation, 5. 2

P. 90 1. 7, 2. 4, 3. 10, 4. 2, 5. 3, 6. 11, 7. 10, 8. 4, 9. cities, 10. logging, 11. mountains, United States, 12. ships, America 13. rivers, America 14. water power, water

P. 91 Subjects and facts will vary. Students should use their own words.

P. 92 1. Center City, 2. Triangle Corners and Oblongville, 3. Diamond Shores

P. 93 1. Bird Pen, 2. East, 3. South, 4. Horse Corral, 5. Armadillo Pen

P. 94 Notes should include: each fall, migrate 3,000 miles, Pribilof Islands to southern California

P. 95 Migrating Monarch Butterflies
I. Migrate south from Canada and Northern United States
II. Spend winter in southern United States and Mexico
III. Return home in spring

P. 96 Topic sentences will vary, but should be complete sentences. Examples for Migrating Swallows: 1. Migrating swallows fly long distances to get away from the cold., 2. Migrating swallows migrate by day., 3. Migrating swallows travel 10,000 miles., Examples for Migrating Geese: 1. Migrating geese live in the United States and Canada., 2. Migrating geese fly in groups. 3. Migrating geese fly as far south as Mexico.

P. 97 Research reports will vary. Students should show each step of process: notes, outlines, rough drafts, and final report with title and good paragraphs.

P. 98 Unit Eight Assessment: 1. Holland, 2. It spoke to her., 3. Shoes can not talk., 4. Madeline could go to Holland with her family. 5. She ran into a shop that sold wooden shoes., 6. People probably will not believe her., 7. She could show people the things that spoke to her and see if they would speak again., 8. Answers will vary.

P. 100 1. b, 2. c, 3. d, 4. a

P. 102 1. a. he ate his food from a plate, b. he did not get dirty, 2. a. he is a pig, b. he looks like a pig, c. he lives with pigs, 3. He wanted to be special., 4. He found out acting differently did not make him special./The other pigs made fun of him./He realized he was special without acting differently.

P. 104 Sarah Spider eats insects and does not fly., Both Sarah and Beth are friends., Beth Bee pollinates flowers, lives in a hive, and can fly.

P. 106 1. c, 2. a, 3. c, 4. a

P. 108 1. d, 2. a, 3. c, 4. c

P. 110 1. underline People came from near and far; circle they wanted to admire and buy the candlemaker's candles., 2. underline The candlemaker gave his candles away, circle he enjoyed making them so much that it did not seem right to ask people to pay for them., 3. underline The candlemaker went to see the woodcutter, circle he had run out of supplies to make candles, and people would need the light from their fires., 4. circle the people wanted the candlemaker to keep making candles, underline they brought him more tallow and dye., 5. circle the people brought more tallow and dye, underline the candlemaker was surprised and pleased.

P. 112 Answers will vary. Possible answers: 1. No, because it was dangerous., or Yes, because they were only near the woods and not in them., 2. No, because they should leave wildlife alone., or Yes, because they might learn something about deer., 3. No, because bears will chase a person who runs., or Yes, because it was dangerous to be near the bear., 4. Answers will vary.

P. 114 Answers may vary slightly. Possible summary: Milly the mouse wanted the Swiss cheese that was on the table, but she did not see Jep the cat. She ran from Jep and hid in the cheese. While she was hiding she ate a lot of cheese and Jep fell asleep. Then Milly ran back to her mouse hole.

Pp. 115-116 1. c, 2. a, 3. b, 4. c

Pp. 117-118 1. d, 2. b, 3. c, 4. d

Pp. 119-120 1. Howard was a very shy little turtle., 2. Howard's mother was determined to make him less shy., 3. The meadow is full of all kinds of animal life., 4. Judy loves to come to the meadow in all the seasons.

Pp. 121-122 Answers will vary. Examples: 1. John got a bicycle that he loved for his birthday., 2. John and his best friend rode their new bikes together., 3. Ginny loved to go shopping for new school clothes., 4. Ginny thought she would not like her little sister to come shopping, but she decided that she didn't mind.

P. 124 1. F, 2. F, 3. F, 4. R, 5. R, 6. R, 7. F, 8. R, 9. F, 10. F, 11. R, 12. R

P. 126 1. She needed a way to stay warm., 2. She usually heated her cottage with wood., 3. There was no wood left to buy., 4. She knits a huge sweater and wraps it around her cottage., 5. Answers will vary.